Cooking
UP A
Storytime

Cooking UP A Storytime

Mix-and-Match Menus for Easy Programming

SUSAN ANDERSON-NEWHAM

An imprint of the American Library Association
CHICAGO 2014

SUSAN ANDERSON-NEWHAM has been the early learning supervising librarian at Pierce County Library in Washington State since 2006. Before that she was a children's reference librarian in King County (Washington). She has also been a professional storyteller, performing at bookstores, local schools, libraries, and other venues. Her bachelor's degree was in developmental psychology, and she completed her MLIS at the University of Washington in 1998. She is an active member of ALSC and PLA as well as several national associations that promote excellence in early childhood education. She has written two humorous pieces for *Children and Libraries* and is the editor of the Pierce County Library *Early Learning Newsletter*.

Printed in the United States of America
18 17 16 15 14   5 4 3 2 1

Extensive effort has gone into ensuring the reliability of the information in this book; however, the publisher makes no warranty, express or implied, with respect to the material contained herein.

ISBN: 978-0-8389-1203-4 (paper).

Library of Congress Cataloging-in-Publication Data

Anderson-Newham, Susan.
    Cooking up a storytime : mix-and-match menus for easy programming / Susan Anderson-Newham.
        pages   cm
    Includes bibliographical references and index.
    ISBN 978-0-8389-1203-4 (pbk.)
    1. Children's libraries—Activity programs—United States. 2. Libraries and preschool children—United States. 3. Storytelling—United States. I. Title.
    Z718.3.A53 2014
    027.62'50973—dc23
                                                                        2013038855

Book design by Kim Thornton in the Minion Pro and Gotham typefaces.
Cover illustration © Avian/Shutterstock, Inc.

♾ This paper meets the requirements of ANSI/NISO Z39.48-1992 (Permanence of Paper).

contents

WEB

Supplemental materials, including full-page
patterns, are available at **alaeditions.org/webextras**

This book is dedicated to my mother and father, Mike and Andy Anderson—thank you for seasoning my crazy life with so many stories and so much love.

preface

THE TASTE OF MY GRANDMOTHER'S FRESHLY BAKED BREAD; the sight of my mother's juicy, golden stuffed turkey, fresh from the oven; the spicy, exotic scent wafting over the backyard fence from my Armenian neighbor's barbeque: these food memories connect me with my childhood and the people whom I loved. The preparation and sharing of food is an essential and pleasurable human experience. It is comfort, warmth, and love. But more than sitting down to a great meal, the fun for me was actually being invited *into* the kitchen: perching on a stool, overlooking or being asked to participate in the chopping, sifting, flipping, and stirring; dipping a spoon into the pot; experiencing the sheer delight of tasting—that was heaven. And it was in those kitchens that I realized that exceptional cooking doesn't just happen. It requires observation, training, practice, and passion. It is the culmination of coming to understand ingredients, putting them together in delectable ways, experimenting, and finally, and most importantly, sharing with people you love.

I find many similarities between the preparation of delicious food and the preparation of exceptional storytimes. Passionate children's librarians are rather like great chefs: language provides the ingredients they select, sift, stir, and portion out in perfect servings in order to feed the developing hearts and minds of the young children in their communities. So with that comparison in mind, I've compiled this storytime cookbook, filling it with what I hope will be delicious and nutritious ideas to serve hungry children and the people who care for them.

The first chapter covers the basics: an overview of the knowledge and experience that will help make storytime creation developmentally appropriate, culturally sensitive, and packed with opportunities for learning. The second chapter provides ideas for rethinking storytime planning in order to maximize the learning opportunities for the children and caregivers in attendance. The subsequent chapters offer a wide variety of storytime ingredients—books, fingerplays, flannelboards, games, poetry, and math and science activities. And the book concludes with a series of "menus" for storytimes.

The focus of this book is predominantly the creation of preschool storytimes, and the menus largely reflect that. My hope is that you, dear readers, will use the ideas in this book as starting points for creating the tastiest storytimes possible, thus continuing to make your libraries vital, cherished, and essential centers of your early learning communities.

acknowledgments

I WOULD BE REMISS IF I DIDN'T BEGIN THE ACKNOWLEDGMENTS WITH a thank-you to Judy Nelson: boss, friend, mentor, and fellow sojourner in the early learning world. This book would never have happened without your insistence and encouragement; lucky Pierce County Library System to have you. A fond thank-you to Stephanie Zvirin: editor extraordinaire—patient, warm, and funny. May we never run out of napkin tricks! To the library staff at Pierce County Library who processed about a billion holds for me, thus making all the menus possible—thank you. And finally to my family: Sally and Robert Favors, for the many enjoyable at-least-once-a-month meals we have shared; Genevieve Pullum, for steadfast encouragement; and especially Mick and Evelyn Newham—amazing husband and beautiful daughter—we share a truly splendid feast.

Storytime Stew

Begin with knowledge and understanding of how children learn and grow

Spend time thoughtfully planning

Select high-quality, entertaining, and age- and audience-appropriate picture books

Mix with a generous assortment of rhymes, fingerplays, stories, songs, and stretchers

Add
- A dash of games
- A sprinkling of poetry
- An ounce of math
- A measure of science

Fold in a healthy heaping of interactivity—ideas to actively engage the children

Add the unique talents of a passionate librarian

Let it sizzle

Serve lovingly to children, parents, and caregivers

Let the feasting begin!

PART 1

Cooking Lessons

1

Understanding How Children Grow and Learn

IF LIBRARIANS HOPE TO PARTNER EFFECTIVELY WITH EARLY LEARNING PRO-fessionals, it's vital that we possess an overall knowledge of child development and our potential role in helping children become ready for school.

Libraries and Early Learning

Storytimes are one of the most enduring, beneficial, and popular programs that libraries offer. And with very good reason: library patrons of all ages attend storytimes. A wonderful portion of the library collection is featured and circulated there. Parents and caregivers discover information, entertainment, and community when they attend storytimes. But most importantly, the story room is an ideal setting in which to introduce children to the incredible world of language, stories, and books. It is where we can help prepare them for successful school experiences. And set them on the path to becoming curious, compassionate, and lifelong learners.

Our world is abuzz with burgeoning research about the developing brain and the importance of the first few years of a person's life. We now understand that the experiences of those first few years have enormous ramifications for a person's physical, social, and intellectual health for the *rest of her life*. Community organizations of all sorts, researchers, health departments, educational service districts, parent groups, tribes, service organizations, child care facilities, preschools, school districts—all are uniting in the understanding that if we work together, we can help change children's lives for the better. Children's librarians can, and should, be critical partners in these growing early learning collaborations. We have a long and rich tradition of programming for young children, but to be considered essential partners in these growing coalitions, we must dedicate ourselves to becoming what I like to call *seasoned librarians*—those who have not only an encyclopedic knowledge of the best books, authors, and resources but also a strong understanding of how children think, grow, and learn. So I begin this book with an overview of important ideas to ponder as we plan programs for our communities—rather like cooking lessons would be for people who want to prepare healthy gourmet meals for the folks who sit down at their table.

Early Learning Contexts

Our understanding of how children grow and develop has deepened and clarified, thanks to more accurate and abundant measurement methods and tools. This insight has helped us better articulate the types of activities and environments that are most beneficial for discovery and learning. There are two vital concepts to keep in mind as we look closely at children's learning and development: one, that children learn *best* in the context of caring relationships, and two, that in everything we plan, we should consider the *whole* child—body, mind, and heart.

When a trusting relationship exists with another person, the richest learning can occur. Indeed, for children under two years of age, learning happens almost *entirely* in that context, which is one of the main reasons the American Academy of Pediatrics recommends no screen time at all for children under two (American Academy of Pediatrics 2011). Several studies have now demonstrated that babies' brains are wired to scrutinize, imitate, and engage other humans *face-to-face*. And even though preschoolers can learn from many mediums, the human relationship remains the most powerful. For the learning that happens is not just language, letters, and concepts, but the deep knowledge of what it means to be a loving human being.

Our storytimes give us wonderful opportunities to establish warm, trusting relationships with children and their families. As young children grow, they move out gradually from the circle of their family to test relationships in the larger community. When we librarians learn children's names and engage them in conversation (and, most especially, *listen* to them when they speak with us), we show the children that they are important to us and that we care about them and their families. Week after week, as they attend storytimes, we establish a relationship with them. This interaction not only broadens their circle but also models how caring adults in the world behave. Children's sense of trust builds. And when they feel trust and a sense of belonging, not only are they empowered for further exploration but the library becomes an optimal place for learning to occur. Therefore, I believe it's best to really focus on human interaction at our storytimes. Today's children have a plethora of opportunities in which to engage technology and fewer and fewer chances to engage loving and receptive people.

As for planning programs with whole-child appeal, our storytimes easily do this (and have done so for over one hundred years!). We engage the children physically through the use of fingerplays, bouncers, stretchers, movement, and dance. We can engage the children's minds by sharing a wide variety of beautiful and interesting books and stories and by asking open-ended questions that encourage conversation about what we have shared. It is through our selection of books and activities that we can spur wonder about our world.

Wonderful stories appeal to children's hearts as well. They may recognize themselves in the unfolding events and sympathize with the characters. Perhaps they are touched by the story. This learning helps build emotional vocabulary and understanding, both essential components in the development of empathy, compassion, and perspective taking.

If we put these two research themes together—the importance of relationships and consideration of the whole child—it seems to me that if we really want to create rich, heartfelt learning at storytimes, we should offer as many interactive opportunities for the children as possible. It is through interaction that they will truly engage in learning with us, with their caregivers, and with other children. It is also through interaction that we can grasp what they understand and what they don't. The more opportunities there are for participation, interaction, and even assessment during storytimes, the more vital the storytimes will be for our children and their families. And that is why interaction is at the heart of this book. I believe storytimes should be loads of fun, but I also believe they can provide children a chance to ponder, test, and practice what they see, hear, feel, and think.

How Young Children Learn

Research into early learning and the testimonies of experienced teachers reveal that very young children often take longer to process new information and questions than do older children and adults. Thus, if we add more interactive elements to storytimes, we should be prepared to give the children plenty of time to process a question posed, formulate an answer, and respond. Some experts have recommended slowly counting to five after posing a question, which may not sound like much but can feel like an eternity when we are not used to it! The active brains of young children are busy making connections but are not very adept at it. If we practice patience, we give them the opportunity to really think something over and then sculpt that thinking into a response or observation. For example, when we hold up the cover of a book we are preparing to read and ask the children, "What do you see in this picture?" we should wait silently but encouragingly for a few moments before prompting a response. That silence allows the children to truly study the cover illustration and ponder and then produce a response.

We can also scaffold learning at storytimes by connecting new information to information that is already familiar to the children. That way we are placing the new information into a context with which they are already at ease and feel safe. This framework makes the new information easy to process. After reading a story about rain, for instance, we can engage the children in a discussion of their own experiences with rain. Do they remember being out in the rain? Where were they? What happened? What did it feel like? How were they dressed? Was it similar to what happened in the story? How was it different? Engaging the children's own experience makes the interaction much more productive (and fun!).

This concept of looking for ways to connect potentially new information to previously mastered information is especially helpful when talking about emotions. The more children are able to talk about and examine the large emotions that they feel, the easier it is for them to eventually gain control over those emotions.

And finally, it's vital to remember that each of us is born with a unique temperament. Some of us are intrepid explorers, some are shy observers, some need a lot of time to adapt to change, some adapt almost immediately. Keeping temperamental differences in the forefront of our minds can be especially helpful with highly interactive storytimes. This awareness supports us by removing our egos from the interactions and keeping the focus on the children's interests and engagement. It's not that this child doesn't like me or is not properly amused at my hilarity. It might simply be that this child's temperament causes him to be cautious around new people and new information; knowing that, I can respond warmly and appropriately.

Family and Culture

Each baby is born into a specific family and culture. Every child grows up in an environment unique to her. As representatives of public libraries, it is our civic obligation to not only respect but *welcome* people who are from cultures different from our own. But how exactly do we do this effectively? Especially when we are serving families from not just one or two but perhaps a myriad of different cultures? I think we might begin by closely examining ourselves and our own culture. What language do we speak? In what sort of environment did we grow up? In what sorts of activities do our friends and families frequently participate? What are our likes and dislikes? What are our pastimes? How do we dress ourselves? What sorts of books, music, movies, and information sources do we like or dislike? What sorts of foods do we like or dislike? What was the extent of our education? What does our standard vocabulary sound like? If we take the time to examine ourselves in an analytical and nonemotional way, we develop a richer understanding of the role that culture plays in all our lives. This knowledge might make it easier for us to approach people from cultures different from our own not with judgment, but with interest, openness, and warmth.

Building on that awareness, it's important to remember that some people are comfortable with silence, some people are quite vocal, some people sit still, some people feel more comfortable moving. Some people are very comfortable standing very close to another person; some people need more personal space around them. Striving to remain open to and accepting of differences, we stand a better chance of creating programs in which everyone feels welcome.

Materials for Preschoolers

Books

Preschoolers are growing fast and furiously. Their language skills are exploding, and they love participating in songs, rhymes, and stories. Giving them the opportunity to join in and repeat familiar phrases in a book or a rhyme helps them hone these new language skills. Because the listening and comprehension skills of preschoolers grow incredibly from ages three to six, we can begin to share longer, more complex stories. Busier illustrations interest this age group, and they may very well (depending on their individual temperament) spend time studying the illustrations closely. But they will still enjoy the simpler books of toddlerhood. Greater comfort with exploring the unfamiliar means that we can share a wider variety of books, not merely books about familiar people, objects, and places. During the preschool years children will progress from knowing only their own family to learning about different families, different communities, and different cultures. This is a wonderful time to introduce books that look out on our diverse and fascinating world. Preschool storytimes also provide a perfect opportunity for us to help children build essential numeracy and scientific knowledge, so along with nonfiction titles, books with math and science concepts should be staples at storytimes.

Rhymes

All rhymes and fingerplays are welcome in preschool storytimes. Repeating them regularly reinforces vocabulary and phonological learning, and they are also immensely fun! The movement accompanying a fingerplay increases learning as well. If the children are also encouraged to actually *create* the rhyme, yet another layer of learning is added. For in order to create the rhyme, the children must think about the question posed and then use their experiences and imaginations to respond to it. This inventiveness calls for more work by the children and may require more effort on the librarian's part, but it will inspire richer learning and engagement, because the children are more directly involved and because the responses will vary each time. (Children's uncensored responses are usually much more entertaining as well.)

Activities

Although literacy skill building remains in the forefront when adding games to storytimes, learning never happens in a vacuum. As with all storytime components, games and activities should engage the whole child—brain, body, and heart. Storytimes that are filled with opportunities to learn, connect, and have fun are the ultimate goal. Because preschoolers have well-developed language capabilities, it's the perfect time to introduce a wider variety of concrete skill-building games—letter identification, letter and word sounds, writing activities, dramatic play opportunities, and the like.

Executive Function

One of the most important sets of child development skills is what researchers have come to call executive function skills. These are the skills of self-control and self-regulation and include planning, monitoring, problem solving, and exercising working memory as well as the ability to focus attention, resist distractions, follow directions, and adjust to changes. According to the Harvard Center on the Developing Child, "Having executive function in the brain is like having an air traffic control system at a busy airport to manage the arrivals and departures of dozens of planes on multiple runways" (Center on the Developing Child 2011). Longitudinal studies have shown that children with excellent executive function skills are much more successful at school and even later in their lives than children with poorly developed executive function skills. And because the critical foundation for executive function skills is developed before age five, librarians should consider these skills keenly as we plan our programs. Our storytimes help children develop attention skills, resist distractions, and even exercise their working memories regularly.

But many of the other executive function skills, such as planning, problem solving, and adjusting to change, are most effectively developed during unstructured, open-ended play with other children. Introducing open-ended toys and a free play portion to our storytimes can provide children an opportunity to exercise their imaginations, create landscapes and scenarios, build, knock down, and build again. They can seek out objects and activities that interest them without interference or undue direction from adults. Engaging in play with others requires children to cooperate and communicate. They use their imaginations to structure the play and must work together to keep it going. This joint effort means talking with each other, working through disagreements, and learning how to compromise. Not falling to pieces because another child is playing with a coveted toy takes a good deal of self-control when you are three or four. And if a child does fall apart, finding herself surrounded by safe, caring adults who help her work through those big feelings is potentially wonderful learning. After all, it is difficult to learn conflict resolution skills if one never experiences conflict!

Adding a play component to a storytime session need not be an overwhelming challenge. It can be as simple as introducing a selection of open-ended toys—blocks, puzzles, dolls, pots, pans, clay, toy cars and toy animals, scarves, capes, and hats—or it can be as complex as assembling themed play boxes that rotate from branch to branch throughout the year.

There is yet another justification for going the extra distance to add a play component to storytimes. A scheduled playtime demonstrates for the parents and caregivers that the library considers play an essential learning tool. It offers the perfect opportunity for librarians to model how to support child-initiated, open-ended, imaginative play. We can also provide materials and resources to help encourage imaginative play outside the library: books about play and research briefs on the importance of play in growing and learning. After all, the impetus for *Every Child Ready to Read* was our recognition that the best way to support children's learning is to support their caregivers with information, modeling, and education.

Every Child Ready to Read

We were given a great gift in 2000 when ALSC (Association for Library Service to Children) and PLA (Public Library Association) rolled out *Every Child Ready to Read*. Learning the underpinnings of early literacy enabled us to speak the language of educators and researchers, adding credibility to what we had already been doing. In addition, the publication gave librarians a strong research base from which to hone and improve storytimes. Understanding the continuum of learning to read—from birth through age eight—and incorporating that understanding into our storytimes form one of the strongest justifications for continuing to have our programs presented by professionals. We are not simply "reading stories" to a group of children. We are fostering the development of language and pre-reading skills, we are promoting every child's right to be ready for school and reading, and we are preparing children for a lifetime love of reading and learning.

The first edition of *Every Child Ready to Read* focused on helping the significant adults in children's lives understand the six skills of early literacy and how to best develop them in the young children in their care. These six skills form the basis of reading readiness: Print Awareness, Letter Awareness, and Phonological Awareness are the decoding skills that children need in order to turn the squiggles on a page into decipherable language. Vocabulary and Narrative Skills are necessary for coming to understand language and ideas and for helping children expand letters and words into thoughts, feelings, and ideas. Print Motivation is an absolutely critical component for creating lifelong readers. We want all children to learn to read easily, but if they stop reading at some point in the future, we have sadly shortchanged them. It is the *love* of print, books, reading, and stories that will keep children, teens, and adults reading throughout their lives.

The second edition of the publication moved from the idea of *what* to build to the idea of *how* to build it. This version made the skill development much more accessible and a seemingly easier task for caregivers. The *five practices* of early literacy included in this version (sing, talk, read, write, play) are still centered on developing the skills needed to become a reader, but for many caregivers, these practices seem less daunting with the educational jargon removed. The new iteration makes skill development at storytimes simpler as well. We already know and have been practicing sharing early literacy skill development with parents and caregivers. Now we may examine our storytime plans and confirm that *all* the practices are present so that we are modeling them for parents and caregivers at each storytime. We may look for additional opportunities for us to talk together with the children. We may add songs or rhyming activities in which the children are encouraged to practice singing or rhyming. We may add a writing component to most sessions, ranging from art activities to name tag creation to pretend or real writing opportunities. We may also look for ways to add more play. As I mentioned earlier, adding an open-ended play component to storytimes is a wonderful way to model the fifth practice of early literacy. It is because of the first edition of *Every Child Ready to Read* that we have the core knowledge and understanding that allow us to more effectively focus on these practices.

Congratulations! You have completed the main cooking lessons in this book. In the next chapter, we will take a brief look at nutritional requirements, and then it will be on to the exciting world of ingredients and recipes!

2

Building Nutritional Programs

THE NEXT STEP IN CREATING RELEVANT AND ENJOYABLE PROGRAMS FOR OUR children and families is to take what we know about how children learn and focus our programs on supporting learning as well as entertainment.

All Dessert, All the Time?

Librarians love presenting storytimes. We thrive on obsessively selecting the perfect developmentally appropriate books, jamming them into themes, hunting down related fingerplays and rhymes and songs, memorizing entertaining and beautiful stories, and looking for ways to be ever more engaging. We craft our own little "Your Favorite Librarian" shows, setting our sights on the satisfaction we feel when our entire storytime group sits enraptured, laughing in all the right places, amazed at our special talents and expertise. And, certainly, having families return week after week and experiencing the increasing devotion that children come to show us seem desirable goals. We want families to attend storytimes! We want strong storytime numbers for our monthly reports! But when we closely examine our offerings in the light of early learning research and standards outside the library walls, is this really the best we can do for the children? Are we offering the most nutritious storytimes possible, or are they perhaps a bit heavy on the dessert side? Can storytimes be more effective in terms of learning for the child and still be highly entertaining? The answer to the last question is undoubtedly yes, but because we know that children learn by doing, we must be willing to involve the children *much* more directly. We must be willing to let go of the "Your Favorite Librarian" solo show and invite the children to come with us into the messy early learning kitchen where feasts are thoughtfully created and joyously (and often sloppily) eaten.

Intentionality

One term that surfaces repeatedly in early learning circles is *intentionality*. Teachers of young children are being encouraged to think deeply about their students' learning. They are urged to be very intentional: set broad goals, stay alert for learning opportunities, introduce concepts, follow the children's lead, observe results, and then evaluate what sort of learning occurred and how they might build and enrich that learning. This seems an excellent light in which to examine our storytimes as well. If we build a storytime around a theme and place our focus on making it highly entertaining, will it contain excellent learning possibilities? Perhaps, but how can we tell? If *we* are doing all the talking during a storytime, is measurement of the children's comprehension, vocabulary, social and emotional development, and overall learning even possible? The research is clear that reading aloud to young children is the most powerful way of developing their understanding and interest in reading. But research is also clear that it is not simply the reading aloud that does the trick. It is the *conversation that surrounds the reading* that has the greatest impact on children's skill development (Dickinson and Smith 1994). If we do all the talking, we may actually be limiting the children's learning!

And that is why we want to invite the children into the storytime kitchen. Because we want them to do more at storytimes, instead of looking for books and activities based on a particular theme, perhaps we should look for books and rhymes that encourage interaction and language skill building. For example, an important pre-reading skill is *retelling*. If we want to focus on the skill of retelling at storytime, what can we do? We can certainly get the children up on their feet to act out a story after they have listened to us read it, but we are still doing most of the heavy lifting there, because *we* are doing the retelling and the children are following our directions for the most part. We have not required them to actually retell anything. A more interactive way might be to look for a book with memorable events, read it aloud in our own unique style, and afterward say, "Let's talk about what happened in this story." This activity can be very challenging for preschool children, as they may need time to truly process a book reading. But if we open the book at the beginning and look at each page together one at a time, and encourage the children to talk about each illustration, we provide them with an opportunity to absorb the story more fully. This strategy is not only a really enjoyable way to talk about the book but also a wonderful modeling exercise for caregivers because it provides plenty of opportunities for dialogue.

Another excellent idea, because children are new to the skill of understanding story, is to scaffold their understanding of the story by setting up the main story points for them *before* we begin reading. For instance, before sharing the book *Inch by Inch* by Leo Lionni, we might say, "In this book, a little worm finds himself in a scary situation. A bird wants to eat him! He has to find some way to fool the bird and get away. Now he's a very clever worm, and so he finds a very clever way to escape. Do you want to read this story together and find out how the little worm gets away from the bird? Let's do!" And then after reading the story aloud, we engage the children in a discussion about how the worm got away and other aspects of the story that they noticed. In this manner, we are deepening their experience with the book, and we are gauging their understanding as well. Sharing thus becomes much more intentional.

Here are some guidelines for incorporating more intentionality in storytimes:

1. Choose each book carefully. Are interactive opportunities embedded in the book itself? For example, does the text pose questions to the reader? If not, at what points in the book might you pose a question or two in order to engage the children more actively and give them a richer understanding of the book? Not so many that you lose the thread of the story, but one or two carefully placed questions to keep the children's interest piqued. I also like to look for at least one book for the storytime that is *very* interactive— we might not even read the text, but just look at the illustrations or photographs and talk about them together. This approach is also an excellent way to incorporate more informational texts into storytime.

2. Read through each book and look for any potentially challenging words. You might introduce and define them before beginning to read. This way you ensure that when the children hear the word during the reading of the story, they won't be distracted by the mystery of it, but will remain engaged with the story instead.

3. Before beginning to read the story, hold up the cover of the book and ask the children, "What do you see?" Ask open-ended questions until the children have established enough about the cover to guess what the book is about. Involving the children in this way not only offers you the opportunity to set up the story but also provides an engaging way to attract the children's attention.

4. If we really want children to have a rich understanding of the stories that we read to them, ideally we should read them more than once. Children love reading the same books over and over (however, their caregivers would

probably stop attending storytimes, and they are usually the ones responsible for transportation!). In place of rereading books, try the retelling scenario mentioned earlier. You can say, "Let's talk about what happened in that story." Then, remembering that it takes children time to process and formulate their thoughts, allow them to ponder. If responses are still not forthcoming, open the book and allow the illustrations to spur their memories. (After all, it's *their* skills that we are hoping to develop!) If I want the children to act out a story after we have read it together, I have them retell it with me in this fashion first and *then* get them up on their feet.

5. Look for math concepts that could be introduced through the book: size, shape, pattern, time, age, distance, comparison, amount—all books contain some mathematical concepts. For example, if you're sharing a book about animals, you could introduce the concepts of big, small, fast, slow, thick, thin, soft, rough, old, young, bright, dull, and so on.

6. What science concepts could be introduced through this book? Look for habitat, life cycle, prey and predator, ecosystems, light and shadow, weather, anatomy, gravity, and the like. For example, after you have shared the book *Fiesta* by Ginger Foglesong Guy, you might bring out a top like the one pictured in the book and ask, "Do you remember this from the book?" Then engage the children in a dialogue about how tops spin. (For large groups, you could demonstrate the top spinning and "wonder" how it is able to keep spinning. Encourage the children to find the answer in the library.) Or after sharing *Hush, A Thai Lullaby* by Minfong Ho, you might go back through the book page by page, point out the creature on each page, and ask the children if that creature lives near them. The creatures featured first are a mosquito and farm animals, which may be familiar to most children, but as the book progresses, the animals become more particular to Thailand, which would open an opportunity to converse about the world's many diverse creatures.

7. Next think about what fingerplays, songs, and stories you want to use and why. You want to include fingerplays that children can imitate and join in on, as well as ones in which they are partners in creation. The fingerplays and action verses written for this book are designed to elicit contributions from the children, thus enhancing their involvement and engagement. Combining these fingerplays and verses with your own collection of incredible fingerplays will provide delicious and nutritious language play for storytime.

8. What connections can you make to the real lives of the children? Have they ever visited a place like the one described in the book? Are their family members similar to characters in the story? Have they ever played in the snow? Dressed themselves? Eaten these foods? Seen that kind of animal?

This process of connecting the stories to the lives of the children enriches their experience with the book.

9. Think about how you might engage more of the children's senses. Can you introduce real items for them to touch and smell? Can movement be incorporated in some way?

This list may seem like a lot of extra work, but it's actually just a change in the way we approach our planning. We certainly don't want to jam every single skill-building possibility into every single storytime, but we can easily add excellent nutrition and interesting seasonings to each meal. And the wonderful part of it is that we don't have to give up the sweets that we love! We are simply creating storytimes that are an entire feast and not simply a single serving of dessert!

PART 2

Stocking
the
Pantry

3

Books

WHEN STOCKING OUR PANTRY FOR STORYTIMES, IT SHOULD BE NO SURPRISE
that books are our first ingredient. They are the sauce for the pasta and the fruit in
the pie!

Ensuring Diversity

Most librarians undoubtedly love sharing new titles with anyone in hearing distance. We adore discovering that a new book is a potential storytime title. We immediately imagine the children laughing. We picture their riveted faces and envision the myriad of connections, art projects, flannelboards, or activities that the book inspires.

Seasoned librarians are aware that the books we choose for storytime are elevated to esteemed status by our families. "*These* are the books my librarian reads to me," the children think. "*These* are the titles I should be sharing with my child," the grown-ups conclude. With that in mind, we should take great care when choosing storytime titles. Do all the books need to be paragons of artistic virtue? Of course not! We want them to reflect the library's collection, the lives of the children, and the world in which we live. After all, libraries are houses of incredible literary diversity, and we want to serve up our collections on silver platters—fiction, informational, funny, poignant, rhythmic, clever, heartfelt, silly, and thought-provoking. Storytime is an ideal place to share these amazing collections with children and their caregivers.

With these considerations in mind, it's critical for us to use the lens of diversity when selecting titles to share. Storytime should be an experience of both belonging and exploring. So the books that we share should work to those ends.

Here are some questions to ponder as you strive for variety and inclusion at storytime:

- Will the children who attend my storytime see themselves reflected in this book?
- Will they find something familiar in this book?
- Will they find something unfamiliar in this book?
- Will they catch a glimpse of the world outside the scope of their day-to-day lives?
- Will this book inspire them to explore an unfamiliar place, idea, or subject?
- Are there steps that I could take or activities that I could introduce to encourage that exploration?
- Is there a healthy variety in the books that I share week to week?

Asking these questions helps ensure that our storytimes are welcoming and enjoyable for everyone.

Here are some wonderful storytime titles that reflect our diverse communities. Titles with asterisks have fewer words per page.

Abuela by Arthur Dorros (Dutton Children's Books, 1991). A young girl and her grandmother sail over their New York City neighborhood.

A-Tisket A-Tasket by Ella Fitzgerald (Philomel Books, 2003). The old rhyme gets a facelift through Ella's jazzy lyrics and the vibrant illustrations.

Bebé Goes Shopping by Susan Middleton Elya (Harcourt, 2006). Wonderful rhyming book about a baby and his mama doing their grocery shopping. The Spanish words sprinkled throughout and the retro illustrations make this a winner.

Bee-Bim-Bop by Linda Sue Park (Clarion Books, 2005). A little girl helps her mother prepare a delicious traditional Korean dinner in this bouncy, happy book.

Bein' with You This Way by W. Nikola-Lisa (Lee and Low Books, 1994). An Impressionist-like celebration of all the ways people look different but are still alike.

Big Red Lollipop by Rukhsana Khan (Viking, 2010). A young girl gets invited to a birthday party and is forced to bring along her little sister. Will appeal to young, school-age children.

Can You Say Peace? by Karen Katz (Henry Holt, 2006). Katz's charming illustrations show children around the world pondering peace.

A Cool Drink of Water by Barbara Kerley (National Geographic Society, 2002). A photographic journey portraying people around the world enjoying a cool drink of water. Gorgeous.

The Empty Pot by Demi (Henry Holt, 1990). A beautiful story set in China about the importance of honesty. Yes, the illustrations are very small, but the story is powerful.

*Feast for Ten by Cathryn Falwell (Clarion Books, 1993). A family shops for groceries and prepares a feast in this wonderful yet simple counting book.

Full, Full, Full of Love by Trish Cooke (Candlewick, 2003). This is a real comfort book whose loving illustrations make it a nice choice for preschoolers.

He's Got the Whole World in His Hands, illustrated by Kadir Nelson (Dial Books for Young Readers, 2005). The old spiritual gets a gorgeous uplift with Nelson's incredible oversized illustrations.

Honey Baby Sugar Child by Alice Faye Duncan (Simon and Schuster Books for Young Readers, 2005). The gorgeous illustrations and abundant love between a mother and her child will appeal to preschoolers.

Honey, I Love by Eloise Greenfield (HarperCollins, 2003). A poetic yet simple look at all the things that a young girl loves. Vivid illustrations will hold appeal for preschoolers and young, school-age children.

Hush, A Thai Lullaby by Minfong Ho (Orchard Books, 1996). The repeating word *hush* makes this lovely book a good choice for quiet times.

*Hush, Little Baby by Brian Pinkney (Greenwillow, 2006). The large and vibrant illustrations, plus the fact that you can sing the book if you like, make this a wonderful choice for storytimes.

I Love Saturdays and Domingos by Alma Flor Ada (Atheneum Books for Young Readers, 2002). A young girl rejoices in her English-speaking family and her Spanish-speaking family.

Is There Really a Human Race? by Jamie Lee Curtis (Joanna Cotler Books, 2006). An amusing look at people all over the world—and a great discussion starter.

Jazz Baby by Lisa Wheeler (Harcourt, 2007). A family celebrates jazz music in this wonderful rhythmic romp. So much fun to read aloud!

Kitchen Dance by Maurie J. Manning (Clarion Books, 2008). A joyfully illustrated story of a family having a night dance in the kitchen—great fun!

*Lola at the Library by Anna McQuinn (Charlesbridge, 2006). The simple story and the adorable illustrations make this book a favorite.

Lola Reads to Leo by Anna McQuinn (Charlesbridge, 2012). Children will enjoy the heartwarming story of big sister Lola reading her favorite books to her new baby brother. The adorable illustrations are sized perfectly for storytime sharing.

Mama, Do You Love Me? by Barbara M. Joosse (Chronicle Books, 1991). A young girl questions the depth of her mother's love in this storytime favorite.

More, More, More Said the Baby by Vera Williams (Tupelo Books, 1990). Three caregivers spend their days playing with babies.

My Grandma / Mi Abuelita by Ginger Foglesong Guy (Rayo, 2007). This very simple book about grandmothers includes mellow, easy-to-see illustrations.

My Mother's Sari by Sandhya Rao (Lerner, 2011). A very simple book about a young girl's impressions of her mother's beautiful sari.

No Dinner! The Story of the Old Woman and the Pumpkin by Jessica Souhami (Marshall Cavendish, 1999). This retelling of an old Asian folktale features many opportunities for repeating phrases. Plus, it's a highly entertaining story.

On Mother's Lap by Ann Herbert Scott (Clarion Books, 1992). A gentle story about a young boy who worries whether there will be enough room on his mother's lap for him now that the new baby is here.

Our Grandparents: A Global Album by Maya Ajmera (Charlesbridge, 2010). Gorgeous photographs from all over the world show children and their grandparents engaging in many activities together.

Papa, Do You Love Me? by Barbara Joosse (Chronicle Books, 2004). A young Maasai boy questions his father about love.

Round Is a Mooncake by Roseanne Thong (Chronicle Books, 2000). Basic shapes are introduced in this vivid book. Grace Lin provides gorgeous illustrations featuring traditional Chinese items.

Say Hello by Rachael Isadora (Putnam, 2010). The diverse city neighborhood, the vibrant illustrations, and the humor will appeal to storytime listeners.

Shades of People by Shelly Rotner (Holiday House, 2009). Attractive photographs of children and delicious vocabulary describing skin tones make this a must-share.

Siesta by Ginger Foglesong Guy (Greenwillow, 2005). Sleepy time is portrayed in this bright and colorful book sprinkled with words in Spanish.

Snow on Snow on Snow by Cheryl Chapman (Dial Books for Young Readers, 1994). Preschoolers will enjoy the spare yet poetic text and the bright, uncomplicated illustrations, but the real star in this lovely book is the gentle, touching story.

Something from Nothing: Adapted from the Jewish Folktale by Phoebe Gilman (Scholastic, 1993). A smooth and entertaining telling of the Yiddish folktale about a boy and his favorite piece of clothing. Bright illustrations complete the package.

Summer Sun Risin' by W. Nikola-Lisa (Lee and Low Books, 2002). Rhyming poems on each page follow a young farm boy from dawn to night on a hot summer day.

Tar Beach by Faith Ringgold (Crown, 1991). A quilt story of a young girl drifting over New York City on a hot summer night.

These Hands by Hope Lynn Price (Hyperion Books for Children/Jump at the Sun, 1999). A simple rhyming book about the many things that hands can do. Large, lovely illustrations are perfect for storytime.

Tortillas and Lullabies / Tortillas y Cancioncitas by Lynn Reiser (Greenwillow, 1998). A lovely book with a repeating verse about four generations of women in a family and how they are alike and how they are different.

Uncle Peter's Amazing Chinese Wedding by Lenore Look (Atheneum Books for Young Readers, 2006). An amusing and authentic look at family, changes, and jealousy!

We March by Shane W. Evans (Roaring Brook Press, 2012). This moving, poetic picture book follows a family as they prepare for the March on Washington, D.C., in 1963 where Dr. Martin Luther King Jr. delivered his "I Have a Dream" speech. The spare yet evocative text and the large and affecting illustrations make this book a wonderful choice to share with a group.

Adding Real-World Flavor

We should all be sharing some factual books at storytime. When you think about it, some of our grown patrons don't read fiction! They may be avid readers, but only of informational books. And if they prefer them, it's highly likely that there are children who attend (or might attend) our storytimes who also prefer nonfiction. The idea that we might be discouraging these children by only using storybooks is disheartening to say the least. Perhaps it's time to overcome our preference for fiction (if indeed we have one) and begin to hunt down factual gems to share. Informational books can work beautifully for storytime even if they seem "too long"—we simply share them differently.

Here are some easy ways to "get real" at storytime:

1. After reading a fictional book at storytime, show a photograph or illustration from an informational title and ask the children questions like these:
   - "What is this?"
   - "Did you see anything like this in the book we just shared? You did? What was it doing? What happened?"
   - "What does this sound like, look like, smell like, taste like?"

2. Use the photographs or illustrations to increase the children's vocabularies.
   • "What is this?"
   • "This is called a barn. It's a sort of house for farm animals. Let's all say that together. Barn. People build barns for their farm animals, but many animals build their own homes."
   • "What do we call this animal's house? Does anyone know?"
   • "Has anyone ever seen one of these?"
   • "Where did you see it?"
   • "What did it smell like?"

3. Use selected parts of a photograph or illustration to encourage children to relate the concepts to their own lives. Ask questions such as these:
   • "This is a photograph of a dolphin from this book titled *Dolphins* by Seymour Simon." (This book is too long to share at storytimes but has wonderful, large photographs—as do most of Mr. Simon's books.) "Have you ever seen a dolphin before? Where did you see it?"
   • "Where do dolphins live?"
   • "Have you ever seen a giant squid?"
   • "Has anyone ever seen fish swimming? Where did you see them?"
   • "I went to an aquarium once. Does anyone know what that is? Yes, it's an enormous tank of sea water filled with fish and other sea creatures."

4. Use the photographs in an informational book to underscore the factual basis of a picture book—for example, a factual book about chickens can enhance the sharing of a Minerva Louise title.
   • "Look! This chicken is walking around in the snow just like Minerva Louise! Do you think she's looking for a hat as well?"

The following are some wonderful informational books that work well at storytime:

The Animal in Me Is Very Plain to See by Laurie C. Tye (WestWinds Press, 2005). Nice photographs and a spare format in which emotions are described and types of animals are pictured. The visual nature of this book might help some children put names to certain feelings.

Animals in Winter by Martha E. H. Rustad (Capstone Press, 2009). Evocative full-page photographs accompany simple text for a nice storytime read.

The Apple Pie Tree by Zoe Hall (Scholastic/Blue Sky, 1996). A lovely book that follows an apple tree through the year and finishes with a recipe for apple pie. Yum!

Arf! Beg! Catch! Dogs from A to Z by Henry Horenstein (Scholastic, 1999). A simple alphabet book of dogs with large and alluring photographs. Perfect for discussion!

The Book of ZZZs by Arlene Alda (Hyperion Books for Children, 2005). Large full-page photographs populate this look at the many ways animals and people sleep. Perfect for sharing with toddlers or preschoolers.

Clothes in Many Cultures by Heather Adamson (Capstone Press, 2007). This very simple book features full-page photographs of clothing worn for a variety of purposes.

A Cool Drink of Water by Barbara Kerley (National Geographic Society, 2002). A photographic journey portraying people around the world enjoying a cool drink of water. Gorgeous.

The Cutest Critter by Marion Dane Bauer (Adventure Publications, 2010). This is a perfect title to use at storytimes. Large, full-page photographs accompanied by simple text introduce children to many different animals. And it rhymes!

Do You Know about Reptiles? by Buffy Silverman (Lerner, 2010). Large photographs and simple yet interesting text make this a nice choice for sharing.

Families by Ann Morris (HarperCollins, 2000). Large photographs of families around the world combined with simple text make this an enjoyable read for preschool storytimes.

Growing Colors by Bruce McMillan (Lothrop, Lee and Shepard, 1988). This book is so simple, only one word per page, but the photographs just beg for conversation. A gem for all ages.

Hair by Nicola Whittaker (Gareth Stevens, 2002). The entertaining photographs and accessible text make this a great choice for reading in its entirety at storytimes.

I'm a Seed by Jean Marzollo (Scholastic, 1996). This easy reader makes a great storytime book as it follows two seeds trying to discover their futures.

My Five Senses by Margaret Miller (Simon and Schuster Books for Young Readers, 1994). Very simple text, wonderful photographs, and lots of possibilities for interaction make this a perfect storytime book.

Pattern Fish by Trudy Harris (Millbrook Press, 2000). This wonderfully fun book is ideal for storytimes. The pattern is established on a double-page spread featuring some sort of sea creature. The children are prompted to complete the pattern when that page is turned. Hilarious illustrations.

Plant Patterns by Nathan Olson (Capstone Press, 2007). Oversized photographs of plants and gardens and very simple text mean this book can be nicely shared in its entirety at storytime. Nice for discussion as well.

Rah, Rah, Radishes! A Vegetable Chant by April Pulley Sayre (Beach Lane Books, 2011). A great storytime book thanks to its beautiful photographs of vegetables far and wide and its accompanying rhyming chant.

Road Builders by B. G. Hennessy (Viking, 1994). A wonderful storytime book that follows the machines and workers building a road. This would also be a great nonfiction companion to *Goodnight, Goodnight, Construction Site*.

Sea Shapes by Suse MacDonald (Harcourt Brace, 1994). Each page begins with a shape and then grows frame by frame into a seascape. The large, colorful illustrations are perfect for storytime.

Senses on the Farm by Shelley Rotner (Millbrook Press, 2009). The attention drawn to the senses makes this a really memorable book to use at storytime. The accompanying photographs are terrific.

Shades of People by Shelley Rotner (Holiday House, 2009). This wonderful book approaches the idea of color by looking at photographs of children with different skin tones. The vocabulary is wonderful too.

Spikey, Slimy, Smooth: What Is Texture? by Jane Brocket (Putnam and Grosset, 1997). This book features large, evocative photographs of many items of differing textures. The embedded questions make this a wonderful interactive read for storytime.

Tender Moments in the Wild: Animals and Their Babies (Moonstone Press, 2001). The two-page photo spreads in this sweet book will work even for large storytimes. Very simple text and the gentle subject matter make this a comforting read.

This Train by Paul Collicutt (Farrar, Straus and Giroux, 2001). Simple text, lots of repetition, and some wonderful math words make this a winner for storytime. Collicutt has many books on different modes of transportation done in this simple style—*This Rocket, This Truck, This Boat, This Plane,* and more.

A Walk on the Beach by Jo Waters (Raintree, 2006). A very simple book filled with photographs of objects one might find at the beach. Wonderful for reading all the way through at storytime.

We Are All Alike . . . We Are All Different by the Cheltenham Elementary School Kindergartners (Scholastic, 1991). This wonderfully interactive book of photographs and illustrations looks at the many ways we are alike and different.

What Is Taste? by Jennifer Boothroyd (Lerner, 2010). An easy nonfiction book (part of a series on the senses) that would be fun at storytime. It features vivid photographs and interesting information. Even grown-ups will learn something.

Who Has These Feet? by Laura Hulbert (Henry Holt, 2011). This vibrant book shows a pair of feet across a two-page spread and then the animal to which the feet belong on the next two-page spread. Simple text and embedded interaction make this a storytime must!

Zoo Pairs by Patricia Whitehouse (Heinemann Library, 2002). An excellent book that examines the concept of pairs. The photographs of animals and the easy text make this a nice choice for preschool storytimes.

Singing Stories

Singing is one of the most effective and enjoyable ways to help children hear the smaller parts in words. It automatically breaks words up into syllables. And it slows down pronunciation allowing the individual sounds to be highlighted. Plus, song lyrics most often rhyme! These are all excellent ways to build the phonological decoding skills that are a necessary part of being ready to read. Children don't care if you can carry a tune or not, but if self-consciousness is going to keep you from singing at storytimes, then by all means use a CD or iPod and encourage everyone to sing along!

To inspire more music at storytime, here are some wonderful books that will encourage singing:

A You're Adorable by Buddy Kaye (Candlewick, 1994). Martha Alexander's sweet illustrations really help bring this wonderful book to life. If you don't know the tune, there is a wonderful *Sesame Street* video of it on YouTube!

All the Pretty Little Horses: A Traditional Lullaby, illustrated by Linda Saport (Clarion Books, 1999). Lovely, muted illustrations and a soft lullaby make this a nice choice for a gentle storytime book.

A-Tisket A-Tasket by Ella Fitzgerald (Philomel Books, 2003). The old rhyme gets a facelift through Ella's jazzy lyrics and the vibrant illustrations.

Cat Goes Fiddle-I-Fee by Paul Galdone (Clarion Books, 1985). The old cumulative song is accompanied by Galdone's wonderful illustrations in this classic for preschoolers.

Down by the Bay by Raffi (Crown, 1987). Nadine Bernard Westcott's amusing illustrations make this a fun and silly title to share.

Down by the Station by Will Hillenbrand (Harcourt Brace, 1999). In this appealing version of the song, the little engine picks up baby animals from all over town (including the children) and drops them at the zoo.

Five Little Ducks by Raffi (Crown, 1989). The well-known song features wonderful illustrations by Jose Aruego. (Raffi has many more songbooks.)

Five Little Monkeys Jumping on the Bed, illustrated by Eileen Christelow (Clarion Books, 1989). This song counts backward from five, children love singing and jumping along, and that is what we affectionately call *playing with numbers.*

Going to the Zoo by Tom Paxton (Morrow Junior Books, 1996). This wonderful book encourages the children to imitate all the animals at the zoo. And it can be sung!

How Much Is That Doggie in the Window? by Iza Trapani (Gareth Stevens, 1999). The classic song in adorable book format. (Iza Trapani has many more songbooks.)

Hush, Little Baby by Brian Pinkney (Greenwillow, 2006). The large and vibrant illustrations, plus the fact that you can sing the book, make it a wonderful choice for storytimes.

Hush Little Baby by Sylvia Long (Chronicle Books, 1997). The old song gets a nature-based reworking in this lovely book. The adorable rabbit illustrations and the gentle bedtime theme will appeal to storytime audiences.

Hush Little Baby: A Folk Song with Pictures by Marla Frazee (Browndeer Press, 1999). The old song, deftly and amusingly illustrated, will find new fans and spur a desire for repeated readings.

Hush Little Digger by Ellen Olson-Brown (Tricycle Press, 2006). This funny retake on the mockingbird song features many different working vehicles.

If You're a Monster and You Know It by Rebecca Emberley (Orchard Books, 2010). A crowd-pleasing, interactive, singing update of a classic—this is such fun to share!

If You're Happy and You Know It by Anna McQuinn (Barefoot Books, 2009). Wonderfully illustrated version of the song with many different movement prompts for a wiggling storytime!

If You're Happy and You Know It, illustrated by Jane Cabrera (Holiday House, 2005). The large and vibrant illustrations stand out in this version of the popular song.

If You're Hoppy by April Pulley Sayre (Greenwillow, 2011). This retooling of the ubiquitous song has great illustrations and fun information and is a blast to sing at storytime.

Inch by Inch: The Garden Song by David Mallet (HarperCollins, 1995). Simple illustrations and a wonderfully singable song make this a winner for spring.

Itsy Bitsy Spider by Lorianne Siomades (Boyds Mills Press, 2001). This is a nice, colorful yet very simple version of the song.

I've Been Working on the Railroad, edited by Ann Owen, illustrated by Sandra D'Antonio (Picture Window Books, 2003). An interesting introduction and the use of just one verse make this a nice addition for storytimes with a wide age range among the attendees.

Los Pollitos Dicen / The Baby Chicks Sing by Nancy Abraham Hall (Little, Brown, 1994). Choose one of the singing rhymes from this wonderful book to share.

Mary Had a Little Lamb by Sarah Hale, illustrated by Tomie dePaola (Holiday House, 1984). The adorable illustrations make this a nice choice for sharing.

Peanut Butter and Jelly: A Play Rhyme by Nadine Westcott (Dutton, 1987). This chanting book features an old rhyme, amusing illustrations replete with elephants, and a repeating line for participation. (Nadine Westcott has many more songbooks.)

Pete the Cat: I Love My White Shoes by Eric Litwin (Harper, 2010). It introduces color, it rhymes, you can sing it, children adore it—this one is a keeper, indeed.

Rah, Rah, Radishes! A Vegetable Chant by April Pulley Sayre (Beach Lane Books, 2011). A great storytime book thanks to its beautiful photographs of vegetables far and wide and its accompanying rhyming chant.

The Seals on the Bus by Lenny Hort (Henry Holt, 2000). A hilarious send-up of the "Wheels on the Bus" song. This one will have everyone at storytime laughing!

Spider on the Floor by Bill Russell, illustrated by True Kelley (Crown, 1993). The book is small in format, but the illustrations are oversized in relation and so wonderfully silly that they deserve to be seen. Plus, you can sing the whole thing!

Ten in the Bed, illustrated by Jane Cabrera (Holiday House, 2005). The old song is accompanied by large, vivid illustrations.

Ten in the Den by John Butler (Peachtree, 2005). A book you can sing, with detailed and adorable illustrations.

There Was an Old Lady Who Swallowed a Fly by Simms Taback (Viking, 1997). Taback's wonderful illustrations and easy text will encourage children to sing along.

There Was an Old Monster by Rebecca Emberley (Orchard Books, 2009). Vivid illustrations on a black background are the perfect accompaniment to this hoot of a book.

This Land Is Your Land by Woody Guthrie, illustrated by Kathy Jakobsen (Little, Brown, 1998). The detailed folk art illustrations may be too intricate for full storytime sharing, but this song can carry the book.

To Market, To Market by Anne Miranda (Harcourt Brace, 1997). A wonderful retelling of the old song with riotous illustrations by Janet Stevens.

Today Is Monday by Eric Carle (Philomel Books, 1993). The old song accompanied by Carle's wonderful cut-tissue illustrations. This is a good one to sing.

We're Going on a Bear Hunt by Michael Rosen (Margaret K. McElderry Books, 1989). Helen Oxenbury's wonderful illustrations make this a great book to chant at storytime.

Encouraging Writing

The phrase "Babbling is talking, chewing is reading, and scribble is script" is often heard in early learning environments. It reminds us that learning is a process. As librarians, we want to give children opportunities to practice and transform their babbling to talking, their chewing to reading, and their scribbling to script. When we introduce writing materials to storytime and encourage the children to use them in meaningful ways, we are providing *contextual* learning experiences that will likely have more meaningful impact. And because writing is one of the five practices of early literacy, the encouragement of writing *belongs* at storytime. Here are some fun ideas to make writing a more integral part of storytime:

1. Create a Storytime Mailbox. This feature may be used as a regular part of storytime. For example, the children can check the mailbox for messages and letters. Library staff members can write notes or postcards to introduce other staff members to the children. You can provide note cards or party invitations for the children and their caregivers to write on. Let the children "send" these cards by putting them into the Storytime Mailbox. If you use a puppet or stuffed animal at storytime, encourage the children and caregivers to write notes to the puppet.

2. Create books by stapling together pieces of paper. Set out magazine clippings, glue, markers, crayons, pencils, and the like and encourage the children to create their own books. Read the books together. Ask, "What's happening on this page?" Or say, "Tell me about this picture . . . " and so on.

3. Cut out words from magazines or print words on the computer and cut them up to create a sort of storytime magnetic poetry. Use the flannelboard for the poetry or encourage the children to paste the words onto pieces of paper. When the series of words is read aloud, they may be nothing more than nonsense verses, but then, nonsense verses are often highly entertaining.

4. Create and write a giant love letter or valentine during storytime. Decide to whom you would like to write—a character from a book or a real person. Post a large piece of paper or a large valentine and let the children suggest what to write.

5. Have your staff compose notes to the children (these could be general letters suitable for any child) and post them around the room ahead of time. (Or put them in your Storytime Mailbox.) Talk about them together or encourage the families to explore the room and read them.

The following are enjoyable books for storytimes with even more ideas for extensions and writing activities:

Bear's Picture by Daniel Pinkwater (Houghton Mifflin Company, 2008). This tongue-in-cheek book about a nonconformist bear and two judgmental gentlemen is a delight to share at storytime.

Bunny Cakes by Rosemary Wells (Dial, 1997). All children deserve to hear a story featuring Max and Ruby. Not only is this story funny, it lends itself to a follow-up writing activity: using a large poster board, create a giant story-time grocery list together. What items would children really like to buy? As the children call out items, write them on the list.

Can You Guess? by Margaret Miller (Greenwillow, 1993). The large photograph of a mailbox can be used effectively in a storytime about letters and the mail.

Carlo Likes Reading by Jessica Spanyol (Candlewick, 2001). This very simple book's illustrations are so packed with labels that it becomes a writing lesson all on its own. There are some wonderful opportunities for interaction as well. Create oversized "labels" with card stock or cardboard, a hole punch, and yarn. Ask the children to identify items in the room—chairs, tables, doors, coatracks, and the like. Create labels for the items and tie the labels onto the objects. Or perhaps create Carlo-type labels to use as name tags.

Children Make Terrible Pets by Peter Brown (Little, Brown, 2010). Amusing illustrations and a tongue-in-cheek story make this an entertaining choice for storytime. Talk about how the author used dialogue "bubbles" to tell the story. Create some silly dialogue bubbles of your own and use them during storytime or the playtime after. Occasionally use drawings or photographs in the dialogue bubbles so the children can be in on the joke as well.

Click, Clack, Moo: Cows That Type by Doreen Cronin (Simon and Schuster Books for Young Readers, 2000). Duck's use of a typewriter to secure special comfort for the farm animals is a riot. After sharing the book, engage the children in a conversation about their experiences with typewriters. Have they ever seen one before? Where? Have they ever used one? If possible, place the typewriter in a place where the children can interact with it after storytime.

Dear Bunny by Michaela Morgan (Scholastic/Chicken House, 2006). This is an adorable story about two bunnies in love. Letter writing and the ripped-up and rearranged sentences may prompt some fun learning activities. Rather long for young groups, but it's too charming to omit. Create valentines and let the children paste tender words onto them.

Giggle, Giggle, Quack by Doreen Cronin (Simon and Schuster Books for Young Readers, 2002). Duck is back in this hilarious book that features many handwritten notes. Talk with the children about how we use notes to each other. Have they ever seen a note? Hang note paper around the room and let the children "write" notes of their own.

Henry Works by D. B. Johnson (Houghton Mifflin, 2004). This story might be rather sophisticated for many storytime groups, but it could spark interesting discussion about authors and writing. Engage the children in a conversation about what an "author" is.

I Miss You Every Day by Simms Taback (Viking, 2007). Vibrant illustrations and rhyming text that repeats make this a great book for storytimes. Pull out the brown paper and boxes, and let the writing begin.

Letter to Amy by Ezra Jack Keats (Harper and Row, 1968). This classic book features an alluring story and wonderful illustrations. The letter at the center of the story offers an opportunity to explore written materials. Engage the children in a conversation about writing letters and about their experiences with receiving or sending letters. Talk about the form that letters take. Provide a template of a letter as a takeaway for the children, or encourage them to write a letter or draw a picture or do both for someone special. If possible, provide envelopes. Talk about stamps and why we use them.

My Crayons Talk by Patricia Hubbard (Henry Holt, 1995). Cute illustrations, simple text that rhymes, colors and crayons—follow a reading with a crayon activity for a very fun storytime. Hang or spread out a big piece of paper—the bigger, the better. Set out crayons or paint (if you're brave) and let the children explore their own pictures and hear their own crayons "talk." Celebrate their efforts. Post this same paper at future storytime sessions and let new children add their art.

Patrick Paints a Picture by Saviour Pirotta (Frances Lincoln Children's Books, 2007). The large illustrations and the embedded interactive guessing game make this a wonderful book to share. And if you are brave, set up a painting activity after sharing.

Secret Valentine by Catherine Stock (Bradbury Press, 1991). A small book in format but with a loving and heartfelt message that children deserve to hear and see. (As long as you can read it without crying!)

Fostering Interaction and Repetition

The last portion of this chapter is about books that encourage children to actively participate. Some of the books are filled with questions aimed directly at the children. Others contain repeating lines. With a little practice beforehand or with some encouragement during the reading, children may join in the repeating line. This repetition not only is very enjoyable for the children but can often assist in maintaining their attention to the story. The following book titles are wonderful for storytime and have built-in interaction or repeating phrases that will encourage the children to "read" along. Titles with asterisks have fewer words per page.

The Baby Beebee Bird by Diane Redfield Massie (HarperCollins, 2000). The baby beebee bird's call begs children to call along. This would be a fun book to act out after a reading.

Bear Feels Scared by Karma Wilson (Margaret K. McElderry Books, 2008). Not only is there repetition to hold the children's interest, but there is strong emotion as well. A great discussion starter.

Bear Snores On by Karma Wilson (Margaret K. McElderry Books, 2002). Children will enjoy watching the action around the sleeping bear and joining in the refrain. A fun story.

Bein' with You This Way by W. Nikola-Lisa (Lee and Low Books, 1994). Cumulative and lyrical text about the ways we are alike and the ways that we are different.

The Bridge Is Up! by Babs Bell (HarperCollins, 2004). The repeating line "Everyone has to wait" and the vivid illustrations will hold the children's attention in this cute book about transportation.

Brown Bear, Brown Bear, What Do You See? by Bill Martin (Henry Holt, 1992). This classic basically reads itself.

Busy Little Squirrel by Nancy Tafuri (Simon and Schuster Books for Young Readers, 2006). The repeating refrain "He was so busy" and the beautiful illustrations make this a wonderful choice to share with children in the autumn.

Can You Guess? by Margaret Miller (Greenwillow, 1993). A question is posed on each page, and four possible answers appear on the opposite page. Children enjoy the silliness of the possibilities and the chance for guessing.

Can You Make a Scary Face? by Jan Thomas (Beach Lane Books, 2009). This book has it all—simple text, bold illustrations, embedded movement prompts, and a large dose of hilarity. Highly interactive!

Come Out and Play, Little Mouse by Robert Kraus (Mulberry Books, 1995). The repetitive phrase in this book also draws attention to the days of the week, making this a nice choice for storytime.

Dance Away by George Shannon (Greenwillow, 1982). The repeating refrain in this book is a set of dance steps. The children might enjoy dancing along with this book.

Dear Zoo by Rod Campbell (Little Simon, 1983). Children enjoy the many "wrong" pets sent to the little boy who is searching for the perfect pet. Plus, the repeating line offers a chance for children to join in.

Do You Want to Be My Friend? by Eric Carle (Crowell, 1971). The simplicity of this book makes it a wonderfully interactive title for storytime—there is a lot of room for questions, answers, and discussion.

Do Monkeys Tweet? by Melanie Walsh (Houghton Mifflin, 1997). Children will enjoy this simple book of silly questions.

Does a Kangaroo Have a Mother Too? by Eric Carle (HarperCollins, 2000). The text is very simple with engaging, repetitive lines, and the bright illustrations provide many opportunities to talk about the various animal mothers as well.

Don't Worry Bear by Greg Foley (Viking, 2008). The little bear's worry and the repeating text make this a nice book for storytimes.

Drummer Hoff by Barbara Emberley (Prentice-Hall, 1967). The repeating line and the humor of this Caldecott winner make it a nice choice.

Froggy Gets Dressed by Jonathan London (Viking, 1992). Preschoolers enjoy the repetitive and often hilarious exchange between Froggy and his mother.

Goodnight, Goodnight, Construction Site by Sherri Duskey Rinker and Tom Lichtenheld (Chronicle Books, 2011). A rhyming story about construction vehicles getting ready for "bed."

Hattie and the Fox by Mem Fox (Bradbury Press, 1986). The hen's observation of a nose, eyes, ears, and so on and the repeated reactions of the other farm animals will easily hold the interest of preschoolers at storytime.

Have You Seen My Cat? by Eric Carle (Simon and Schuster Books for Young Readers, 1987). Wonderful repeating sentence and Carle's signature cut-paper illustrations make this a great choice for storytimes.

A House Is a House for Me by Mary Ann Hoberman (Viking, 1978). This wonderful, exhaustive book about houses may be too long for many storytimes, but portions of it would work beautifully, and the repeating line may help focus straying attentions.

I Ain't Gonna Paint No More by Karen Beaumont (Harcourt, 2005). Not only does this book have a repeating line for audience participation, but it also is filled with rhyming completion prompts!

I Am Small by Emma Dodd (Scholastic, 2010). A wee penguin enjoys being small because the love his parents feel for him is large. This is a smallish book in format, but the illustrations are vivid and nice for storytime, and children will enjoy the repeating text.

"I'm Not Cute" by Jonathan Allen (Hyperion Books for Children, 2006). The frustration that baby owl feels at constantly being labeled "cute" will surely hold familiar appeal for young children.

It's Funny Where Ben's Train Takes Him by Robert Burleigh (Orchard Books, 1999). A rhyming story about a young boy and the train adventures that he creates for himself. Features a repeating line.

Jump, Frog, Jump! by Robert Kalan (Greenwillow, 1981). The text builds page by page, and children are invited to call out the repeated warning to the frog. Children enjoy jumping along with this book.

Just Like Daddy by Frank Asch (Prentice-Hall, 1981). The simple story and the repeating phrase make this a nice choice for toddlers and preschoolers, and mommies and daddies will snicker or cringe at the surprise ending.

*Kitty's Cuddles by Jane Cabrera (Holiday House, 2007). The large, bright illustrations, the questions, and the many different animals make this a cuddly, interactive winner for storytime.

Little Donkey Close Your Eyes by Margaret Wise Brown (HarperCollins, 1995). Rhyme, repetition, and beautiful woodcut illustrations make this a lovely, gentle choice for storytime.

Mama, Is It Summer Yet? by Nikki McClure (Abrams Books for Young Readers, 2010). A little boy repeatedly asks if it's summer yet in this lovely book for preschoolers.

*Meeow and the Pots and Pans by Sebastien Braun (Boxer, 2010). Large, bright illustrations, simple text, and an amusing mystery of a story make this a storytime winner. The direct questions embedded in the text will naturally draw interaction from the children. Create a storytime band after the reading for extra fun.

Millions of Cats by Wanda Gág (Coward, McCann, 1988). This simple, classic book deserves to be read by all children.

Mother, Mother, I Want Another by Maria Polushkin Robbins (Crown, 1978). The misunderstanding between a mother and her baby at bedtime is an entertaining read for storytime.

Mothers Are Like That by Carol Carrick (Clarion Books, 2000). This beautifully illustrated book shares the qualities of many animal mothers and features a repeating line.

Muncha! Muncha! Muncha! by Candace Fleming (Atheneum Books for Young Readers, 2002). Children will enjoy the antics of the rabbits and the lengths to which the farmer goes to deny them his garden.

The Napping House by Audrey Wood (Harcourt, 1984). The text in this wonderful book is cumulative, and children will enjoy joining in as the story unfolds.

No Dinner! The Story of the Old Woman and the Pumpkin by Jessica Souhami (Marshall Cavendish, 1999). This retelling of an old Asian folktale features many opportunities for repeating phrases. Plus, it's a highly entertaining story.

Noisy Nora by Rosemary Wells (Dial, 1973). Rhyming text and a few repeating lines make this a nice read-aloud at storytimes.

Pie's in the Oven by Betty G. Birney (Houghton Mifflin, 1996). The refrain will have everybody hungry for pie by the book's end. Delicious!

Press Here by Herve Tullet (Chronicle Books, 2011). This wonderful exploration of color and directions can make for an active storytime. Children can take turns following the instructions on each page, or everyone can act them out from his or her seat. Fun!

Sleep, Big Bear, Sleep! by Maureen Wright (Marshall Cavendish Children, 2009). The antics of the bear who mishears a message from Old Man Winter will greatly amuse children.

Someone Bigger by Jonathan Emmett (Clarion Books, 2004). This wonderful book features rhyming text, a silly story, and an easy phrase for repeating (as well as a nice message about never being too small to make a difference).

Something from Nothing: Adapted from a Jewish Folktale by Phoebe Gilman (Scholastic, 1993). The easy telling of this story and the built-in repetition will engross older preschoolers and young, school-age children.

Te Amo, Bebé, Little One by Lisa Wheeler (Little, Brown, 2004). A mother sings a repeating song to her baby as he grows in this sweet book.

Ten in the Den by John Butler (Peachtree, 2005). This retelling of the ten in the bed song features terrific vocabulary and adorable illustrations. A crowd pleaser.

Trashy Town by Andrea Zimmerman (HarperCollins, 1999). The repeating chant in this book, the appealing illustrations, and the accessibility of the story make this a storytime favorite.

Watch Out! Big Bro's Coming! by Jez Alborough (Tundra Books, 2005). An easy-to-remember repeating line, hilarious illustrations, and the amusing ending make this a great candidate for preschool storytime.

Who Ate All the Cookie Dough? by Karen Beaumont (Henry Holt, 2008). Children may repeat this question long after the story is over. This is a fun book with wonderful, vibrant illustrations.

*Who Hops? by Katie Davis (Harcourt Brace, 1998). The built-in questions, lively illustrations, and silly humor make this a fun storytime book.

*Whoo? Whoo? by David A. Carter (Little Simon, 2007). The die-cut illustrations function as the main prompt for interaction and discussion in this clever book, making it a nice choice for smaller storytimes when everyone can see the pages clearly.

*Whose Hat? by Margaret Miller (William Morrow, 1997). The hat photographs in this book make an interactive guessing game for both toddlers and preschoolers.

*Woof! Woof! by David A. Carter (Little Simon, 2006). The same format as *Whoo? Whoo?* with dogs as the main characters. A nice choice for smaller storytimes. Plus, it's funny!

Would You Rather? by John Burningham (Crowell, 1978). Though this may be a bit long for many storytime children, the silly choices posed on each page make it a highly interactive and very entertaining book to share in part at storytimes.

Wow! Said the Owl by Tim Hopgood (Farrar, Straus and Giroux, 2009). The bright, colorful illustrations, the repeating line, and the charming story of a little owl experiencing the daytime for the first time make this a favored storytime choice.

Language Play

THE NEXT ESSENTIAL INGREDIENTS FOR OUR STORYTIME PANTRY ARE THE rhymes and fingerplays that enhance our children's love for words and language.

Language and Learning

Seasoned librarians practice the rich library tradition of sharing fingerplays and action verses with young children and their caregivers. Our library shelves are filled with volumes of delightful verses to use with children, and with access to the Internet, it's as easy to find entertaining fingerplays, action verses, and stretchers as it is to type "fingerplays cows" on the keyboard. As we know from the research behind *Every Child Ready to Read*, these verses increase vocabulary skills, narrative skills, phonological awareness, listening skills, and knowledge about the world. Plus, they are really, really fun! Preschool children learn a great deal through imitation, and the fingerplays that we employ are wonderful for encouraging imitation. When we repeat their rich vocabulary and incorporate movement, song, or chant, we literally bathe children in language.

Incorporating more interaction into our language play with children, asking the children themselves to make more of a contribution, will add even more to their learning. By asking for their contribution, we ask them to listen to the question posed, ponder an answer, relate it to what they already know, brainstorm ways to contribute, and finally articulate their idea to the group. This is very active learning! Plus, when the children are part of the creation, the verse will constantly change and can therefore be repeated many times and still be fun. And contributions from the children are often quite inventive, making the storytime more enjoyable for adults as well!

A Potful of Words

The following are interactive fingerplays and action verses that invite contributions from the children.

Action Words
>I can stand. (*stand*)
>Can you stand? (*encourage children to stand*)
>I can sit. (*sit*)
>Can you sit? (*encourage children to sit*)
>Stand, sit.
>Stand, sit.
>We can stand and sit!

What else can we do? (*Take suggestions from the children. Pick two new actions.*)

>I can _____ (*one of the actions suggested*).
>Can you _____?
>I can _____ (*the other action suggested*).
>Can you _____?
>_____, _____.
>_____, _____.
>We can _____ and _____!

(*Repeat until everyone is exhausted!*)

Autumn
>What is the season?
>What is the season?
>What is the season?
>Do you know?

(*Encourage the children to name the season.*) How can you tell when it's autumn? What do we see in the world outside that makes us think of autumn? (*Choose one observation and insert it into the chant. For example,* we see the red leaves *or* we see the leaves fall *or* we see the pumpkins.)

> We see the leaves fall,
> We see the leaves fall,
> We see the leaves fall,
> That means autumn!
>
> We see the pumpkins . . .
> We feel the cold air . . .
> We feel the wind blow . . .

Bugs in the Yard

> It is so nice to wander (*mime walking*)
> All around the yard.
> The grass is soft and fuzzy, (*wiggle your fingers like grass*)
> And the rocks are hard. (*bump your knuckles together*)
> We look up at the sky, (*look up*)
> We look down on the ground. (*look down*)
> And suddenly . . . oh! (*point*)
> A bug's been found!
> Oooh! What is it? (*look more closely*)

What kinds of bugs might we see outside? (*Choose one of the suggestions.*) What does a _____ look like? Does it fly? Has anyone else seen a _____?

> It is so nice to wander (*mime walking*)
> All around the yard.
> The grass is soft and fuzzy, (*wiggle your fingers like grass*)
> And the rocks are hard. (*bump your knuckles together*)
> We look up at the sky, (*look up*)
> We look down on the ground. (*look down*)
> We've already found a _____,
> And . . . oh! (*point*)
> Another bug's been found!
> Oooh! What is it?

(*Take more suggestions and choose one.*)

> It is so nice to wander (*mime walking*)
> All around the yard.

The grass is soft and fuzzy, (*wiggle your fingers like grass*)
And the rocks are hard. (*bump your knuckles together*)
We look up at the sky, (*look up*)
We look down on the ground. (*look down*)
We've already found a _____ and a _____,
And now what bug's been found? (*point*)

(*Keep repeating until you have a long list of bugs, then:*)

It is so nice to wander (*mime walking*)
All around the yard.
The grass is soft and fuzzy, (*wiggle your fingers like grass*)
And the rocks are hard. (*bump your knuckles together*)
We've seen so many bugs,
They crawl and hop and fly.
But now it's time to go inside
And so you bugs, good-bye!

Bugs Move

This chant is very active as you act out each of the bug activities together. There are no wrong ways to act out the bugs. Just have fun. You can extend the learning by initiating discussion about the bugs either before or after the chant.

Spiders in the yard they
spin, spin,
spin, spin,
spin, spin.
Spiders in the yard they
spin, spin,
On a sunny day.

Butterflies they
flutter, flutter,
flutter, flutter,
flutter, flutter.
Butterflies they
flutter, flutter,
On a sunny day.

Bees in the yard they
buzz, buzz,
buzz, buzz,
buzz, buzz.
Bees in the yard they
buzz, buzz,
On a sunny day.

Beetles in the yard they
click, click,
click, click,
click, click.
Beetles in the yard they
click, click,
On a sunny day.

Worms in the yard they
slither,
slither,
slither.
Worms in the yard they
slither,
On a sunny day.

Ladybugs they
flit, fly,
flit, fly,
flit, fly.
Ladybugs they
flit, fly,
On a sunny day.

Slugs in the yard they
chew, munch,
chew, munch,
chew, munch.
Slugs in the yard they
chew, munch,
On a sunny day.

Dragonflies they
dip, dive,
dip, dive,
dip, dive.
Dragonflies they
dip, dive,
On a sunny day.

Fireflies they
blink, blink,
blink, blink,
blink, blink.
Fireflies they
blink, blink,
On a summer night.

Mosquitos they
eeeeee, bite,
eeeeee, bite,
eeeeee, bite.
Mosquitos they
eeeeee, bite,
Ouch! Time to go inside!

Down at the Seaside

Down at the sea side
The waves roll in, (*roll hands like waves*)
The sun shines over the sea. (*form a circle overhead*)
Under my umbrella I am sitting (*form an umbrella shape with your arms*)
Naming the things I see.

Look! Up there in the sky! A long, white bird is flying and calling out loudly. What kind of bird could that be? (*Take suggestions.*) Has anyone ever seen a _____? What were you doing? What was it doing?

Down at the sea side
The waves roll in, (*roll hands like waves*)
The sun shines over the sea. (*form a circle overhead*)
Under my umbrella I am sitting (*form an umbrella shape with your arms*)
Naming the things I see.
I saw a _____ flying overhead.

What else do you think I would see at the beach? (*Take suggestions and pick one.*)

> Down at the sea side
> The waves roll in, (*roll hands like waves*)
> The sun shines over the sea. (*form a circle overhead*)
> Under my umbrella I am sitting (*form an umbrella shape with your arms*)
> Naming the things I see.
> I saw a _____ flying overhead.
> I see a _____. (*name another object*)

What else might I see at the beach? (*Keep taking suggestions and repeating until the children are ready to move on.*)

The Farmer

> The farmer tills her field, (*model tilling*)
> She plants her rows of seed. (*pretend to drop seeds into rows*)
> She tends them and waters them (*mime watering*)
> So they will grow and feed . . .
> US!

Farmers grow some delicious food. Can you think of a food that farmers might grow? (*Choose one suggestion from the children.*)

> The farmer tills her field, (*model tilling*)
> She plants her rows of seed. (*pretend to drop seeds into rows*)
> She tends them and waters them (*mime watering*)
> So they will grow and feed us _____! (*fill in suggested crop*)

What else would you like the farmer to plant?

> The farmer tills her field, (*model tilling*)
> She plants her rows of seed. (*pretend to drop seeds into rows*)
> She tends them and waters them (*mime watering*)
> So they will grow and feed us _____ and _____. (*fill in suggested crop*)

What else should the farmer plant? (*Repeat until the children are ready to move on.*)

Feelings

>Inside of us are feelings,
>They all live right inside. (*cross your hands over your heart*)
>They may be tall, (*stretch your arms up*)
>They may be small, (*make a small gesture with your fingers*)
>Narrow, or wide. (*put hands close together and then stretch them out wide*)
>Sometimes they show a little,
>Sometimes they show a lot!
>We have so many feelings, can you name one that we've got?

We've got sadness sometimes. It looks like this: (*show a sad face, weep a bit, and so on*). Shall we try another one? What is another feeling that we feel? (*Choose one.*) What do we look like when we feel that feeling?

>Inside of us are feelings,
>They all live right inside. (*cross your hands over your heart*)
>They may be tall, (*stretch your arms up*)
>They may be small, (*make a small gesture with your fingers*)
>Narrow, or wide. (*put hands close together and then stretch them out wide*)
>Sometimes they show a little,
>Sometimes they show a lot!
>We've got sadness . . . (*repeat the sad face*)
>We've got _____. (*use the chosen emotion and act it out broadly*)
>What's another one we've got?

What is another feeling we sometimes have? What do we look like when we are feeling that way? (*Keep repeating, adding on more and more emotions and showing or talking about what they look like when we feel them.*)

Getting Dressed

This is sort of a dancing story. Get everyone up on their feet for lots of silly action.

>We want to get dressed and go outside and it's cold, cold, cold!
>What do we need to put on if we want to go outside? Clothes!
>But what clothes should we put on?

(*Encourage the children to call out items, or simply suggest pants first.*)

Put on our pants, pants, pants,
They make us dance, dance, dance! (*dance around or at least move your feet*)
We love our pants, pants, pants!
We love to dance, dance, dance!
And then, what do we need to put on?

(*You may take these in any order, but here are the rhymes and movements that accompany the items of clothing.*)

Put on our shirt, shirt, shirt.
Look! There's some dirt, dirt, dirt.
We'll change our shirt, shirt, shirt,
One without dirt, dirt, dirt.

We've got our pants, pants, pants!
And we will dance, dance, dance!
We've got our shirt, shirt, shirt,
One without dirt, dirt, dirt.
What should we put on next?

Put on our socks, socks, socks,
They give us shocks, shocks, shocks! (*wiggle your feet*)
Sometimes our socks, socks, socks,
Will give us shocks, shocks, shocks!

We've got our pants, pants, pants!
And we will dance, dance, dance!
We've got our shirt, shirt, shirt,
One without dirt, dirt, dirt.
We've got our socks, socks, socks,
That give us shocks, shocks, shocks.
What should we put on next?

Put on our shoes, shoes, shoes,
They come in twos, twos, twos.
We count our shoes, shoes, shoes,
First one, then twos, twos, twos.

We've got our pants, pants, pants!
And we will dance, dance, dance!

We've got our shirt, shirt, shirt,
One without dirt, dirt, dirt.
We've got our socks, socks, socks,
That give us shocks, shocks, shocks.
We've got our shoes, shoes, shoes,
First one, then twos, twos, twos.
What should we put on next?

Put on our hat, hat, hat,
Give it a pat, pat, pat.
Our funny hat, hat, hat.
It likes a pat, pat, pat.

We've got our pants, pants, pants!
And we will dance, dance, dance!
We've got our shirt, shirt, shirt,
One without dirt, dirt, dirt.
We've got our socks, socks, socks,
That give us shocks, shocks, shocks.
We've got our shoes, shoes, shoes,
First one, then twos, twos, twos.
We've got our hat, hat, hat.
It likes a pat, pat, pat.
We're just about ready, just one more thing to put on because it's cold out-
    side.

Put on our coat, coat, coat.
On it we dote, dote, dote.
We love this coat, coat, coat.
It gets our vote, vote, vote.

We've got our pants, pants, pants!
And we will dance, dance, dance!
We've got our shirt, shirt, shirt,
One without dirt, dirt, dirt.
We've got our socks, socks, socks,
That give us shocks, shocks, shocks.
We've got our shoes, shoes, shoes,
First one, then twos, twos, twos.
We've got our hat, hat, hat.

It likes a pat, pat, pat.
We've got our coat, coat, coat.
It gets our vote, vote, vote.
We are ready! Let's go outside and play!

Good Night Loves

Night has risen, (*gently raise hands*)
Stars are twinkling brightly
In the sky above. (*wiggle fingers above your head*)
I am sleepy, (*mime sleepiness*)
So I'll say good night
To people that I love.

When you are ready for bed, to whom do you like to wish good night? (*Choose one suggestion from the children.*)

Night has risen, (*gently raise hands*)
Stars are twinkling brightly
In the sky above. (*wiggle fingers above your head*)
I am sleepy, (*mime sleepiness*)
So I'll say good night
To _____.
You're my love.

I'm still awake! Is there someone else I should wish good night? (*Choose two suggestions.*)

Night has risen, (*gently raise hands*)
Stars are twinkling brightly
In the sky above. (*wiggle fingers above your head*)
I am sleepy, (*mime sleepiness*)
So I'll say good night
To _____ (*first suggestion*) and _____ (*second suggestion*).
You are both my loves.

Still awake! Who else needs a wish good night? (*Choose suggestions.*)

Night has risen, (*gently raise hands*)
Stars are twinkling brightly
In the sky above. (*wiggle fingers above your head*)
I am sleepy, (*mime sleepiness*)

So I'll say good night
To _____ (*first suggestion*) and _____ (*second suggestion*) and _____ (*third suggestion, and so on*).
You are all my loves.

(*getting somewhat exasperated*) I'm still awake! Who else needs a wish good night? (*If you keep going on long enough, this can get quite humorous with sometimes outlandish suggestions from the children. Finish with:*)

Night has risen, (*gently raise hands*)
Stars are twinkling brightly
In the sky above. (*wiggle fingers above your head*)
I am sleepy, (*mime sleepiness*)
So I'll say good night
To _____ and _____ and _____ and _____ and _____ (*and so on*).
You are all my loves.
(*yawn*) Good night! (*close eyes and snore*)

Grocery Cart

We're off shopping
Down at the mart.
We've got a list
Of things for the cart.

When you go shopping, what sorts of things do you put in your grocery cart? What do you most like to eat? (*Encourage the children to call out items, pick one, and continue.*)

We're off shopping
Down at the mart.
Here is a _____ (*name item chosen*)
To place in our cart.

What else shall we put in our cart?

We're off shopping
Down at the mart.
We put a _____ (*first item*) and now here's a _____ (*name second item chosen*)
To place in our cart.

What else shall we put in our cart?

> We're off shopping
> Down at the mart.
> We put a _____ (*first item*) and then put a _____ (*second item*) and now
>   here's a _____ (*name third item chosen*)
> To place in our cart.

(*Keep going until the list is long or until the children wish to move on. Finish with:*)

> We're done shopping,
> We did our best.
> Let's unpack and have a rest!

Hugs and Kisses

> Grown-ups pinch up my cheeks
> And say that I'm so tall,
> But then they do the thing
> That makes me shudder most of all!
> They give me . . .
>
> Hugs and kisses, (*hug yourself and jump up and down*)
> Hugs and kisses,
> All around my face! (*place hands on sides of face in alarm*)
> Hugs and kisses, (*hug yourself and jump up and down*)
> Hugs and kisses,
> It's simply a disgrace! (*throw arms up in the air*)
>
> Hugs and kisses, (*hug yourself and jump up and down*)
> Hugs and kisses,
> Every single time. (*wag your finger*)
> Hugs and kisses, (*hug yourself and jump up and down*)
> Hugs and kisses,
> Can't they tell that I'm . . .
> Practically . . . grown . . . up! (*place hands on hips in exasperation*)

Can you think of somebody who likes to give you hugs and kisses? (*Pick one answer and begin again.*)

_____ pinches up my cheeks
And says that I'm so tall,
But then she/he does the thing
That makes me shudder most of all!
She/He gives me . . .

Hugs and kisses, (*hug yourself and jump up and down*)
Hugs and kisses,
All around my face! (*place hands on sides of face in alarm*)
Hugs and kisses, (*hug yourself and jump up and down*)
Hugs and kisses,
It's simply a disgrace! (*throw arms up in the air*)

Hugs and kisses, (*hug yourself and jump up and down*)
Hugs and kisses,
Every single time. (*wag your finger*)
Hugs and kisses, (*hug yourself and jump up and down*)
Hugs and kisses,
Can't she/he tell that I'm . . .
Practically . . . grown . . . up! (*place hands on hips in exasperation*)

Who else likes to give you hugs and kisses? (*Continue singing and dancing the Hugs and Kisses song until the group is ready to move on.*)

Hungry Tummy

Hungry, hungry, hear our tummies?
Grrrrooowwl, Grrrrooowwl,
Hungry, hungry, we're so hungry,
We need food right now!

What shall we feed our tummies? (*Encourage suggestions.*)

_____ in our tummies.
Grrrrooowwl, Grrrrooowwl,
Hungry, hungry, we're still hungry,
Need more food right now!

What else shall we feed our tummies? (*Take more suggestions. Finish with:*)

Hungry, hungry, hear our tummies?
Full, full!
We're so happy, oh so happy,
Tummies now are full!
Sigh. (*sit and snore or burp if you like!*)

My Little Kitty

I love my little kitty, (*one hand pets the other*)
She's very soft and sweet.
She likes to play with balls of string, (*roll hands round and round*)
And she loves to eat! (*mime eating—get messy slurping!*)

What else do kitties like to do? (*Encourage suggestions.*)

I love my little kitty, (*one hand pets the other*)
She's very soft and sweet.
She likes to play with balls of string, (*roll hands round and round*)
She likes to _____, (*act out suggested activity*)
And she loves to eat! (*mime eating—get messy slurping!*)

And what is another thing that kitties like to do? (*and so on*)

My Painting

We're making a painting, bright and bold, (*mime painting with a brush*)
We paint on some silver, we paint on gold.
Hmm. (*bring your finger to your chin as though contemplating*)
It needs more color.

What color should we add to our painting? (*Choose a color from the children's suggestions.*)

We're making a painting, bright and bold, (*mime painting with a brush*)
We paint on some silver, we paint on gold.
We've now added _____. (*name of color chosen*)
Hmm. (*bring your finger to your chin as though contemplating*)
It needs more color.

What color should we add to our painting now? (*Choose another color from the children's suggestions.*)

We're making a painting, bright and bold, (*mime painting with a brush*)
We paint on some silver, we paint on gold.
We've now added _____ and also _____. (*names of colors chosen*)
Hmm. (*bring your finger to your chin as though contemplating*)
It needs more color.

What color should we add to our painting now? (*Last time:*)

We're making a painting, bright and bold, (*mime painting with a brush*)
We paint on some silver, we paint on gold.
We've now added _____ and also _____ and also _____ and also _____
   and also _____ and also _____ and also _____ and also _____ and also
   _____. (*names of colors chosen*)
Hmm. (*bring your finger to your chin as though contemplating*)
It's beautiful! We're done!

Numbers Like to Fly

Numbers like to fly
High up in the sky.
Flying round and round my head,
Numbers like to fly.
They fly around me high, (*stretch your arms up*)
They fly around me low, (*reach your arms down low*)
And when they get too close to me
I'll catch one! (*make a grasping motion with your hand*)
Oh, this is a good one! (*Look into your hand as though you are observing the
   number. Choose a number to describe. Then repeat using a different number.*)

Here are some examples:

- 8—This number is round at the top and round at the bottom and crosses in
  the middle. This number is less than 9. This number is more than 7.
- 11—This number looks like two poles side by side. If you're counting, it
  comes before 12. It follows 10.
- 5—This number rhymes with "thrive." This number is less than 6.
- 13—Ooooh. Some people think this number is unlucky. But I think it's
  kind of nice. If you're counting, it comes right before 14. It follows 12.
- 19—This is the last number in the "teens." If you're counting, it comes right
  before 20. It follows 18.

Road Trip

> We're on a road trip, (*jostle steering wheel*)
> We've packed a lunch. (*point to bag*)
> What did we bring to munch, munch, munch?

What would you like to eat at lunch? (*Encourage children to name food items and choose one to begin with.*)

> We're on a road trip, (*jostle steering wheel*)
> We've packed a lunch. (*point to bag*)
> We've brought a _____ to munch, munch, munch.

What else did we bring? (*Add one of these to list.*)

> We're on a road trip, (*jostle steering wheel*)
> We've packed a lunch. (*point to bag*)
> We've brought a _____.
> We've brought a _____ to munch, munch, munch.

What else did we bring? (*Add these to list.*)

> We're on a road trip, (*jostle steering wheel*)
> We've packed a lunch. (*point to bag*)
> We've brought a _____.
> We've brought a _____.
> We've brought a _____ to gulp, gulp, gulp (*when a drink is suggested*) or
>   munch, munch, munch.

What else did we bring? (*Add these to list.*)

Shopping for Food

One day I went to the grocery store to do my shopping. I had a long list of things to buy. First, I chose a . . . a . . . oh, what's that thing called that you push and you toss your groceries into it? What's that called? (*Take suggestions or suddenly remember "cart" or "grocery cart."*) Right! A grocery cart!

So I pushed my *grocery cart* down the . . . down the . . . oh, what's that called? You know . . . that . . . long . . . the grocery store is laid out in them, long . . . you know . . . you walk down it . . . (*Take suggestions or suddenly remember "aisle."*)

Right! I pushed my *grocery cart* down the *aisle* and on the shelf I saw a package of . . . a package of . . . you know, you toast a slice of it for breakfast or you use it for the outsides of a sandwich . . .

Right! *Bread!* So I put the *bread* into my *grocery cart* and kept walking down the *aisle.*

Next I saw a whole shelf of . . . oh, what are they called? . . . They're red or green and crisp and kind of sweet or maybe sort of sour and you can cut them into slices . . . what are they called?

Right! *Apples!* Oh, I love apples, don't you? So I placed a bag of *apples* into my *grocery cart* and kept walking down the *aisle.*

Next I saw a whole shelf of these . . . you know . . . yellow fruit. They're round and their skin is sort of bumpy and when you taste it, your face goes like this (*scrunch up*). You know . . . what are they called?

Right! *Lemons!* I love lemons. You can squeeze them to make a really delicious drink called . . . oh . . . what is that drink called? (*Lemonade.*)

Right! *Lemonade!* So I placed a bag of *lemons* in my *grocery cart* and I kept walking down the *aisle.* (*Continue adding items that would be familiar to the children in your community. When you have played this story out, end with:*)

So at last, my shopping was done, and I took my *grocery cart* up to the . . . the . . . what's that called? Where the nice person slides the groceries across the counter . . . Right! The *checkout!* And the nice person put all my groceries into . . . into . . . you know, those things that you use to carry your groceries home . . . what are they called? Right! *Bags!* And I took all my groceries home, unpacked them, and whew! I was tired. So I lay down on my bed and took a . . . a . . . you know! Right! *Nap!*

Spring

    What is the season?
    What is the season?
    What is the season?
    Do you know?

How can you tell when it's spring? What do we see or feel in the world around us that makes us think of spring? (*Choose one observation and insert it into the chant. For example,* we see the flowers *or* we feel the rain *or* we feel the wind.)

    We see the blossoms,
    We see the blossoms,
    We see the blossoms,
    Which means spring!

We see the flowers . . .
We feel the rain . . .
We feel the wind . . .

Summer

What is the season?
What is the season?
What is the season?
Do you know?

How can you tell when it's summer? What do we see or feel in the world around us that makes us think of summer? (*Choose one observation and insert it into the chant. For example,* we play outside *or* we feel the sunshine *or* we see the fireflies.)

We see the sunshine,
We see the sunshine,
We see the sunshine,
Which means summer!

We play outside . . .
We feel the heat . . .
We see the fireflies . . .

Tippy-Tappy

Here's my little puppy dog, (*wiggle index finger*)
Her name is Tippy-Tappy.
I've given her a bone to chew, (*hold a "bone" up to "Tippy-Tappy"*)
And she seems happy.

RUFF! (*shake finger as though barking*)
Uh, oh. I think she needs something.
What could it be? (*encourage the children to provide answers to what she might need*)

Here's my little puppy dog,
Her name is Tippy-Tappy.
I've given her a bone to chew,
I've given her a _____, (*whatever was suggested*)
And she seems happy.

RUFF!
Uh, oh. I think she still needs something else.
What could that be?

Here's my little puppy dog,
Her name is Tippy-Tappy.
I've given her a bone to chew,
I've given her a _____,
I've given her a _____,
And she seems happy.

RUFF!
Uh, oh. I think she still needs something else.
What could that be?

(*Continue adding things for Tippy-Tappy until this last verse:*)

Here's my little puppy dog,
Her name is Tippy-Tappy.
I've given her a bone to chew,
I've given her a _____,
I've given her a _____,
I've given her a _____,
I've given her a _____,
I've given her a _____,
And now she's finally happy!

RUFF! (*have finger "fall asleep"*)

A Visit to the Farm

Tell the children you are going to tell a story and they are going to make all the noises for it. You may have to scaffold this a bit—give examples of some of the sounds that will be required and practice them together before you begin.

We went to visit a farm one day. Our car went like this on the road (*make bumping movements*). And it sounded like _____. (*If they don't make a sound, ask them, "What does a car sound like?"*)

When we arrived at the farm, the farmer walked out of the barn and said _____. (*Give the children time to answer but if they don't make a greeting, say "Hi!"*) He began to show us around the farm.

There were cows in the barn saying _____.

There was a cat in the barn hunting mice. She looked at us and said _____.

Up in the rafters an owl looked down sleepily upon us. He said _____.

We walked out of the barn and over to the chicken coop. The chickens said _____.

And the little baby chicks said _____.

We picked up a warm egg from the nest. The egg said _____. (*mime holding an egg up to your ear and make a puzzled face*)

Suddenly we heard horses in the pasture. They said _____.

There were dogs chasing sheep in the next pasture. The dogs said _____, and the sheep sounded like this:_____.

Suddenly, we realized we were hungry. Our tummies went _____.

The farmer invited us to lunch. We sat at a picnic table and ate. It sounded like this: _____.

After lunch we felt sleepy. The birds sang in the trees like this: _____.

The farmer fell asleep and snored like this: _____.

We wrote a thank-you note for the farmer like this. (*exaggerate pretending to write a note*)

And we crept back to our car like this. (*mime moving quietly*)

We started our car. And drove home like this. (*mime the drive home*)

Good-bye, Farm! Thank you!

Walking through the Forest

This could easily be made into a movement story if you have a group that can move about the room without difficulty. But it also works standing in place or even sitting.

Walking through the forest on a rainy day, I see a lot of animals along the way. (*mime walking through the forest, rain coming down, and looking for animals*)

This animal is sort of small and sort of round. She has prickly needles all over her skin! What do you think she is? A porcupine! Yes! You are right. A porcupine.

Walking through the forest on a rainy day, I see a lot of animals along the way. (*mime walking through the forest, rain coming down, and looking for animals*)

This one likes to sleep during the day. I might not have seen him at all since he lives up in the treetops, but he has very big, round eyes and he was making this sound . . . "Whooo, whoo." Who do you think he is? An owl! Yes! You are right. An owl.

Walking through the forest on a rainy day, I see a lot of animals along the way. (*mime walking through the forest, rain coming down, and looking for animals*)

I can feel this one watching me from afar. Silent, watching. And then I hear this sound . . . "AaahWoooooo!" Who howls like that? A wolf! Yes! You are right. A wolf!

Walking through the forest on a rainy day, I see a lot of animals along the way. (*mime walking through the forest, rain coming down, and looking for animals*)

(*mime a bad smell*) What's that smell?? This animal is black and white and whoooooeeeee! It smells really, really strong. What animal could possibly make that smell?? A skunk! Yes! You are right. A skunk.

Walking through the forest on a rainy day, I see a lot of animals along the way. (*mime walking through the forest, rain coming down, and looking for animals*)

Oh! This one is very shy and cranky! He's hiding in a hole, and he's growling at me! Wow, look at his teeth! He's not very big, but he sure looks mean! Do you know what he is? A wolverine! Yes! You are right. A wolverine. Let's get away fast!!!

Walking through the forest on a rainy day, I see a lot of animals along the way. (*mime walking through the forest, rain coming down, and looking for animals*)

I hear a lot of noise! Something very, very big is coming! It's grunting and growling, looking for honey. Who is coming? A bear! Bears and wolverines??? (*make a scared face*)

Running through the forest on a rainy day! I'm going to run home all the way! (*mime running*)

This action story was written for children of the Northwest, which is why it's a rainy day! But you could adapt it to the area around your town by substituting animals common to your area.

Who Is in a Family?

Who is in a family? (*put arms out in an "I don't know" sort of gesture*)
Who is in a family? (*point to brain as though thinking*)
Who is in a family? (*put arms back out*)
Do you know?

Can you name someone in a family? (*Encourage children to name someone.*)

There's a *Mommy* in a family, (*for example*)
A *Mommy* in a family,
A *Mommy* in a family,
And who else?

(*Take another suggestion.*)

There's a *Daddy* in a family,
A *Mommy* in a family,
Both are in a family,
And who else?

There's a *Nanny* in a family,
A *Daddy* in a family,
A *Mommy* in a family,
And who else?

There's a *Papa* in a family,
A *Nanny* in a family,
A *Daddy* in a family,
A *Mommy* in a family,
And who else?

(*Repeat until children run out of family members, then finish with:*)

That makes a family,
That makes a family,
That makes a family,
Full of love!

Winter

What is the season?
What is the season?
What is the season?
Do you know?

How can you tell when it's winter? What do we see or feel in the world around us that makes us think of winter? (*Choose one observation and insert it into the chant. For example,* we see the snow *or* we wear our coats *or* we feel the wind.)

We feel the cold,
We feel the cold,
We feel the cold,
Which means winter!

We see the snow . . .
We wear our coats . . .
We feel the wind . . .

Zoo Who?

These are riddles for the children to solve. I like to use a bag with finger puppets of each animal inside, but you could also use small photographs of animals.

My feet are like tree trunks,
My nose like a hose.
I use it to spray off
My back and my toes.
My ears are large,
And my eyes are small,
And I'm almost as wide
As I am tall.
What am I?
(*elephant*)

I'm covered in spots
Like dappled shade.
I'm lean,
And elegantly made.
I nibble leaves
In the African sun.
And my neck
Is longer than anyone's.
What am I?
(*giraffe*)

King of the jungle,
That is my name.
I have powerful claws,
It's true.
My hair is so thick,
They call it a mane.
Take care
If I gaze at you.
What am I?
(*lion*)

I have stripes of black.
I have stripes of white.
Four hooves to run,
If I feel a fright.
I nibble on grass
And leaves of course.

I may look like one,
But
I'm not a horse.
What am I?
(*zebra*)

I like to eat grass
And leaves and bugs,
And you'd never call me dumb!
I swing from trees,
I chitter and scream,
And I have an opposable thumb.
What am I?
(*monkey*)

My skin is rough and scaly.
I can wait for my food
A long while.
And though I have
Impressive teeth,
You should stay
Far away
From my smile!
What am I?
(*crocodile*)

I have a big horn
On the end of my nose
(Though it's mostly made of hair.)
I'm not very smart,
But I'm really quite fierce,
And I *charge*, so you'd better beware!
What am I?
(*rhinoceros*)

Transition Rhymes

Transitioning from one activity to the next can be a challenging feat for young children at storytimes. Transition rhymes can be an excellent way to get standing children back into their seats and ready to listen. Here are some rhymes written for that purpose. The movements to accompany them should be self-explanatory.

I Can Hop

I can hop,
I can leap,
I can clap,
I can sleep.
I can turn around,
I can blow a kiss,
I can sit right down,
Just like this!

Laughing Clap

Laughing clap, (*clap hands*)
Happy slap, (*cross hands to slap opposite shoulders*)
Smart I am with a tap tap tap. (*tap index finger against temple*)
Flying flap, (*flap arms like wings*)
Sleepy nap, (*yawn and drop to the floor*)
Hands I fold in my lap lap lap. (*fold hands into your lap*)

Quivering

I shake my hands
And wiggle my nose.
I jiggle my knees and my elbows.
I wobble my backside
As fast as it goes.
I'll flubber my lips
Then plop on the floor,
And then I'll be ready
To listen some more!

This Is My Head

This is my head,
And these are my toes.
I can turn around twice, I suppose.

Jump up high,
Then sit on the ground.
Shhhhhhh!
Not a sound . . .

5

Flannelboards

WHEN I WAS FOUR, MY MOTHER BELONGED TO A BOWLING LEAGUE. AND WAY back then, the bowling alley offered a nursery school for the children of league bowlers (imagine!). I don't recall the name or the face of the lovely woman who entertained us while our mothers bowled, but I do remember three things about her: her very full, crinoline-lined skirts; her kind and gentle manner; and her astonishing flannelboard. To my four-year-old self, those little figures hanging magically on that fuzzy black board captivated me almost as much as the story or song that accompanied them. I think perhaps I have been obsessed with flannelboards ever since! And I love the idea of using the flannelboard to engage the children in conversation and language play.

Using the Flannelboard

The flannelboard can be used in many ways to develop the early language and literacy skills of young children—to encourage rhyming skills; to introduce concepts such as numbers, counting, and colors; to prompt developing language skills through open-ended questions; even to incorporate movement to help scaffold language learning. This chapter introduces some fun flannelboard ideas and includes patterns.

RHYMING FLANNELBOARDS
Creating flannelboard figures that have rhyming prompts within them encourages the children to participate and allows us to gauge their abilities based on their

responses. We may introduce flannelboards with figures that rhyme or incorporate what are called *completion prompts*. To use a completion prompt, begin a phrase with an embedded rhyme but stop short of completing the rhyme to allow the children to complete it. For example, during a storytime about food, I might say,

"When I am hungry, I stand on my feet,
And walk to the kitchen for something to _____."

Pausing and allowing the children to complete the rhyme makes the learning more active for them and allows us to measure their ability to hear and produce rhymes. The following flannelboards all focus on developing the skill of hearing and producing rhymes.

Child's Face

This flannelboard rhyme is an example of a completion prompt. You can alter the hair to make this figure any child you like or a number of different children.

To make a child in this place
We must put up one, round _____. (*face*)
We will add for some flare
Black, shiny, curly _____. (*hair*)
Because our child will want to hear,
On each side, we'll place an _____. (*ear*)
Our child will want to see the skies,
So we'll add two shining _____. (*eyes*)
So that she can smell a rose,
Let's put here a button _____. (*nose*)
If we put this upside down,
She will wear a lowly _____. (*frown*)
But we want a happy style,
So let's flip it to a _____. (*smile*)
A bow right here and she is done,
Our happy child is ready for fun!

Pattern 5.1

Supplies
- small amounts of felt in colors appropriate for the child you would like to create
- scissors

Directions
Download pattern 5.1 from alaeditions.org/webextras. Using the pattern, cut the face, hair, ears, eyes, nose, smile, and bow out of different colors of felt.

Telling

As you progress through the rhyme, place the appropriate piece on the flannel-board.

Ocean Riddles

This flannelboard is another completion prompt. Place all the objects on the board beforehand and as you say each riddle, remove the object after the children have successfully rhymed. You might want to share an informational book or photographs of the sea objects used here before sharing this story so the children will know the names of the objects you are removing from the flannelboard.

A cloudy day at sea is rather fun, so let's remove the shining _____. (*sun*)
We want a story of undersea words, so let's remove the flying _____. (*birds*)
We want things that do not float, so let's remove the floating _____. (*boat*)
We really want a tiny tale, so let's take off the great big _____. (*whale*)
We think the sea looks much too floral, so let's remove all the _____. (*coral*)
The story is ending as you wish, let's finally remove the school of _____. (*fish*)
It's all gone, how can that be? I suppose it's time to remove the _____. (*sea*)

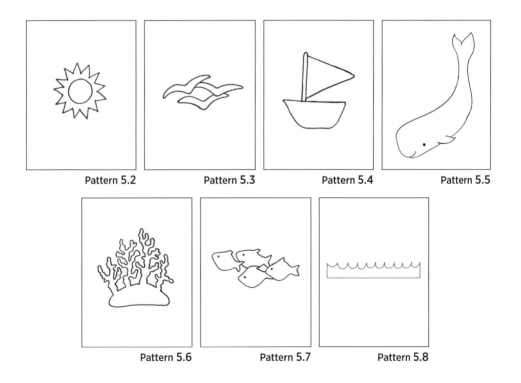

Pattern 5.2   Pattern 5.3   Pattern 5.4   Pattern 5.5

Pattern 5.6   Pattern 5.7   Pattern 5.8

Supplies
- yellow felt (sun)
- white felt (birds)
- brown felt (boat)
- gray felt (whale)
- pink felt (coral)
- green felt (fish)
- blue felt (sea)
- scissors

Directions
Download patterns 5.2 through 5.8 from alaeditions.org/webextras. Using the patterns, cut the sun, birds, boat, whale, coral, fish, and sea out of the chosen shades of felt.

Telling
Arrange all the items on the flannelboard before you begin the story. As you complete each line, pause, allowing the children to choose the appropriate rhyming piece to remove.

The Rat, the Gnat, and the Fine, Fat Cat

This flannelboard is a fun exploration of the "at" sound—great for decoding the sounds of words and determining what they have in common. You may strengthen the children's rhyming skills by turning the story into a completion prompt if you like.

Once there was a cat.
He was actually quite fat.
He wore a tall top hat,
This fine, fat cat.

He had a friend, a rat,
Who held a baseball bat,
And sat upon a mat
Beside the fine, fat cat.

A tiny, noisy gnat
Buzzed around the rat,
Buzzed around the cat,
And buzzed around his hat.

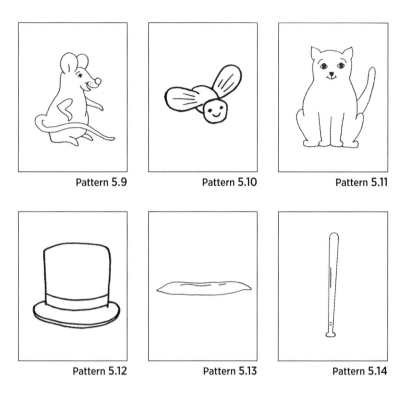

Pattern 5.9   Pattern 5.10   Pattern 5.11

Pattern 5.12   Pattern 5.13   Pattern 5.14

The rat took his bat,
Swung it at the gnat,
But he only knocked the hat
Off the fine, fat cat.
Drat!

Supplies
- small amounts of felt in a variety of colors
- scissors

Directions
Download patterns 5.9 through 5.14 from alaeditions.org/webextras. Using the patterns, cut the cat, rat, hat, bat, mat, and gnat out of your chosen colors of felt.

Telling
With each line, place the appropriate flannelboard piece on the board and pause before naming it aloud, giving the children the opportunity to finish the rhyme. You may move the figures to illustrate the story in the latter portion.

CONCEPT FLANNELBOARDS

The following flannelboards help develop many different conceptual skills.

Bubbles

This is an easy flannelboard song/chant that can be used to focus on counting or color vocabulary.

> I blew one big bubble, (*put a bubble on the flannelboard*)
> I blew one big bubble,
> I blew one big bubble,
> I hope that it won't pop! (*clap once*)
> Pop! (*clap once*)
> Pop! (*clap once*)
> I hope that it won't pop! (*clap once*)
>
> I blew two big bubbles, (*put another bubble on the flannelboard*)
> I blew two big bubbles,
> I blew two big bubbles,
> I hope that they won't pop! (*clap twice*)
> Pop! (*clap twice*)
> Pop! (*clap twice*)
> I hope that they won't pop! (*clap twice*)

(*Keep adding bubbles and counting their pops until you run out of bubbles or the children grow weary of counting!*)

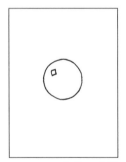
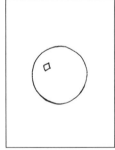
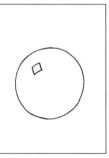

| Pattern 5.15 | Pattern 5.16 | Pattern 5.17 |

Supplies
- felt in one color
- scissors

Directions

Download patterns 5.15 through 5.17 from alaeditions.org/webextras. Create all the bubbles in the same color to clarify the activity for the children. Preschoolers are generally only able to focus on one attribute at a time, and creating bubbles in different colors might make the activity confusing.

Bubbles (Color Alternative)

I blew one big bubble, (*put a bubble on the flannelboard*)
I blew one big bubble,
I liked the color of this bubble,
It was _____. (*encourage children to name the color of the bubble*)

I blew two big bubbles, (*put another bubble on the flannelboard*)
I blew two big bubbles,
I liked the color of these bubbles,
They were _____ and _____. (*continue adding bubbles and naming their colors*)

Supplies

- felt in many colors
- scissors

Directions

Create the bubbles in many different colors, but choose only one size for them all.

Shapes and Colors

Cut out different shapes for the flannelboard. Most preschool children can only focus on one attribute at once, so either put up one shape in many colors (for example, circles in many colors) so you can talk about color, or many shapes in one color (for example, many red shapes) so you can talk about shape. This can also be a wonderful opportunity to develop vocabulary in different languages.

Common Shapes in Spanish	*Common Colors in Spanish*
heart . . . . *un corazón*	red . . . . *rojo*
square . . . . *un cuadrado*	blue . . . . *azul*
circle . . . . *un círculo*	green . . . . *verde*
rectangle . . . . *un rectángulo*	white . . . . *blanco*
oval . . . . *un óvalo*	orange . . . . *anaranjado*
cube . . . . *un cubo*	purple . . . . . . *morado*
pentagon . . . . *un pentágono*	yellow . . . . *amarillo*
triangle . . . . . . *un triángulo*	brown . . . . *café*
	black . . . . *negro*
	gray . . . . *gris*

COUNTING AND SUBITIZING

The flannelboards in this section were created to give children a fun way to practice counting and subitizing. *Subitizing* is the ability to recognize at a glance the number of objects in a set. Think of the dots on the sides of dice. A young child may need to count the dots on the dice to know how many are showing, whereas an older or more experienced child can glance at, for example, five dots and say "five" without having to stop and count. Young children can learn to subitize very well with practice. Storytime flannelboard figures are a perfect medium with which to help children practice this very important foundational math skill.

Counting Puppies

One little puppy dog
Heads out to play.
She leaps and rolls,
Barking, "What a day!"

Pattern 5.18

Another little puppy dog
Heads out to play.
She leaps and rolls,
Barking, "What a day!"
How many puppies are playing now?

(*Point and count aloud and ask, "How many?" again.*)

Another little puppy dog
Heads out to play.
She leaps and rolls,
Barking, "What a day!"
Now how many puppies are playing?

(*Continue counting puppies and asking, "How many?" When all the puppies are on the flannelboard, end with:*)

All these puppies
Have played in a bunch,
And now they are hungry.
It's time for _____. (*lunch*)
Good-bye, puppies!

(*Take each puppy off the board and count backward.*)

Counting Sheep

Here's a little woolly sheep
  (*hold up the sheep in your hand that is opposite*
  the flannelboard)
Who wants to say good night.
Count her leaping over
  (*"leap" the sheep over yourself and place her on*
  the flannelboard)
To help us sleep tight.
ONE!
How many sheep do you see?
You're right, just one!

Here's another woolly sheep
Who wants to say good night.
Count him leaping over
To help us sleep tight.
TWO! (*place the second sheep on the flannelboard next to the first sheep*)
How many sheep are there now?
Let's count them together.
One, two.
How many?

Pattern 5.19

(*Encourage the children to count out loud as you point to each sheep. Each time you finish counting sheep on the board, ask the children, "How many?" This approach helps the children to understand cardinal numbers—the numbers that stand for how many items they see at once.*)

Subitizing Leaves

This flannelboard gives the children practice subitizing without counting. Young children will have better success at subitizing if the number of items is six or fewer. (To work on counting higher than ten, make many more flannelboard pieces.)

One little leaf in the autumn,
Fallen from the tree.
One little leaf in the autumn.
How many do we see?

Pattern 5.20

(*Count the leaf and then ask, "How many?"*)

> Another leaf in autumn,
> Fallen from the tree.
> Another leaf in autumn.
> How many do we see?

(*Count the leaves and then ask, "How many?" Continue to add up to six leaves.*)

Subitizing Snowmen

Here's another flannelboard to help children practice subitizing.

Pattern 5.21

> Here's a snowman standing tall.
> Can we count him, one and all?

(*Count the snowman and then ask, "How many?"*)

> Another snowman standing tall.
> Can we count them, one and all?

(*Count the snowmen and then ask, "How many?" Add up to six snowmen.*)

FLANNELBOARD IDEAS WITHOUT A STORY

Using open-ended flannelboards—those not necessarily tied to a story—allows the children to do the work. When we simply put a piece on the flannelboard and ask "What's this?" we are encouraging children to ponder, recall, and articulate an answer, all of which involves a whole lot more skill building than just watching and listening! Following are some ideas for open-ended flannelboard figures. The flannelboard patterns and ideas presented here were created to maximize interaction and conversation, while focusing on development of various skills.

Family

This flannelboard can be used at storytimes as a vocabulary builder for the names of family members in English and other languages as befits your community. Download patterns 5.22 through 5.28 from alaeditions.org/webextras. The father and mother figures can become aunts and uncles, the brother and sister figures can become cousins or stepbrothers and stepsisters, and so on. You may use them with the rhyme "Who Is in a Family?" (see chapter 4) or on their own as prompts to talk about different types of families. They are designed to stand beside one another holding hands.

| Pattern 5.22 | Pattern 5.23 | Pattern 5.24 | Pattern 5.25 |

| Pattern 5.26 | Pattern 5.26A | Pattern 5.27 | Pattern 5.28 |

Ladybug under the Flower

This flannelboard was inspired by the popularity of "Little Mouse, Little Mouse, are you in the _____ house?" If you are unfamiliar with that flannelboard story, it involves having houses of many colors on the flannelboard with a small mouse hidden behind one house. The storyteller repeats the rhyme, and the children call out the color of the house to pull off the flannelboard in search of the hidden mouse. Children love playing this sort of hidden object game. But in an effort to encourage even more dialogue, using more complex objects means the children must use words more descriptive than just a color name to identify the object they wish removed. This increased dialogue builds vocabulary and incorporates social and emotional skill building, as the children must take turns describing which item to remove.

Download patterns 5.29 through 5.37 from alaeditions .org/webextras. Place all the flowers on the board with the ladybug hidden beneath one. Tell the children that the ladybug is hiding behind a flower and ask where they think she is hiding. Let the children choose which flower to remove first, second, third, and so on.

Pattern 5.29

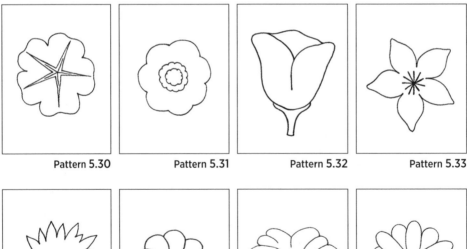

Pattern 5.30

Pattern 5.31

Pattern 5.32

Pattern 5.33

Pattern 5.34

Pattern 5.35

Pattern 5.36

Pattern 5.37

Transportation

One at a time, put a jet, car, boat, truck, scooter, bicycle, hot air balloon, plane, helicopter, rocket ship, horse, submarine, and foot on the flannelboard. After the children have named the figure, ask: "What is it used for?" "Have you ever seen one?" "Have you ever ridden in one?" "Did you use that to get to the library today?" and so on. I like to finish this flannelboard with a boat or a horse and ask how many children used one of those to get to the library. (Perhaps you live in an area where they *would* use a boat or a horse! In that case, choose something that would be an unlikely mode of transport.) This makes the flannelboard funny as well as effective.

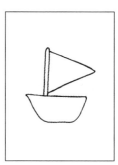

Pattern 5.4

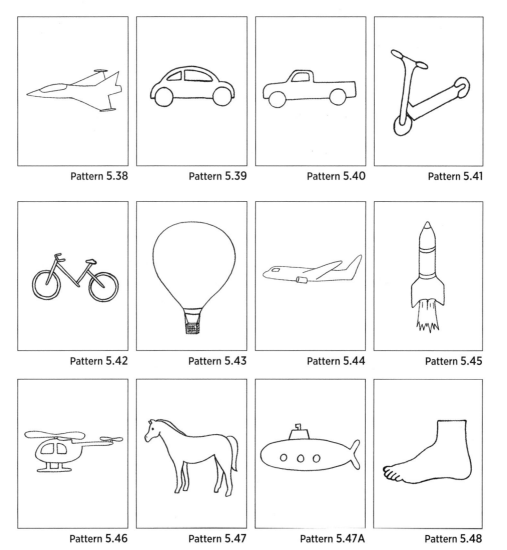

Pattern 5.38   Pattern 5.39   Pattern 5.40   Pattern 5.41

Pattern 5.42   Pattern 5.43   Pattern 5.44   Pattern 5.45

Pattern 5.46   Pattern 5.47   Pattern 5.47A   Pattern 5.48

FLANNELBOARDS WITH MOVEMENT OR HANDS-ON PARTICIPATION

Five Brown Buns

Using traditional rhymes at storytimes connects our modern children to the canon of western literature, plus the rhymes have wonderful vocabulary and rhythm. To add interest and participation to "Five Brown Buns," have five children line up against a wall to the right or left of where you sit. Give them each a penny and place five brown bun pieces on the flannelboard. Sing the rhyme together and encourage the five children, one at a time, to walk across the room, stop to hand you a penny at the appropriate time, and take a bun from the flannelboard. With the entire group, count the buns left on the board and then sing the rhyme again as the next child walks across the room to "buy" a bun. It may seem as though you are singing the rhyme a thousand times (which for large groups may be about right!), but the children and their caregivers really seem to enjoy this activity, and it truly seals the rhyme in everyone's memory.

Pattern 5.49

> Five brown buns in the bakery shop,
> Five brown buns with sugar on top.
> Along came a fellow/gal with a penny in his/her hand,
> He/She took one bun,
> And away he/she ran.

Love Tree

For this flannelboard, place the tree trunk on the board. Pass out a flannelboard piece to each child. You may have to work in groups if you have very large story-times. The pieces might be red and pink hearts for Valentine's Day or assorted green hearts to celebrate the return of spring. Tell the children that when it is their turn to give their "leaf" to the tree, they will say, "Here is my love for Tree" or "Here is a leaf for Tree." Practice that line several times with the children so they are comfortable in their knowledge of it. Then begin the story.

Pattern 5.50   Pattern 5.51

This is Tree. She lives in a beautiful little forest on the edge of town.

She is a young tree and had smiled through the breezy days of summer.

In summer her leaves made little laughing sounds when the wind rustled them. (*Encourage the children to "rustle" their leaves.*)

But days went by and the autumn winds blew, and all the leaves fell from Tree.

More days went by and the winter snows fell.

Through the long winter Tree slept. Softly, softly, softly dreaming.

The days began to grow a bit longer.

The sun began to shine a bit brighter and one day Tree awoke.

(*yawn*) Oh, that was a lovely winter! Soon it will be summer and I will rustle my leaves.

But look at my branches! They are still bare!

Where, oh, where are my leaves?

I feel so lonely without my leaves.

I wonder where they could be?

Does anyone know?

Is there anyone who would help Tree?

Does anyone have a little love for Tree?

(*Encourage the children to come up one at a time and place their leaf on the flannelboard and say, "Here is my love [or "a leaf"] for Tree." When they have all brought their leaves forward, end the story with the following:*)

Oh! Thank you, thank you! Tree feels so beautiful!

Now the birds will land on my branches and build nests.

And the bees will buzz through my blossoms and gather pollen.

And I will stretch my limbs to the summer sun and rustle my leaves all summer long.

Ah!

It's lovely to be Tree.

6

Games

PLAYING GAMES AT STORYTIME ALLOWS US TO INTRODUCE THE ALPHABET, math concepts, science concepts, real-world information, language play, print awareness, phonological awareness, vocabulary—a wealth of possibilities. Plus, games are fun! Games can also help children build many social and emotional skills: taking turns, waiting for a turn, focusing, communicating, troubleshooting, and the like. The following games are meant as a starting point. Build, change, and morph them into games suited to your audience and size of storytime.

Alphabet Hunt

Supplies
- alphabet banner
- individual letters of the alphabet (preferably identical in font and color to the letters on the banner)
- bag or box to hold the letters

Directions
Post the alphabet banner in the room or post individual letters around the room. (Create letters large enough for all the children to see at storytime.) Print a second set for yourself (these could be smaller, but in a font and color that match the larger corresponding letters). Put all the smaller letters in a bag and slap your hand on your thigh as you chant this rhyme:

Hunt, hunt,
An alphabet hunt,
We're going on an alphabet hunt.
The letter _____ (*pull a letter from the bag and call out its name*)
Is hiding its face.
Let's go find its hiding place!

(*Holding up the letter for all to see, choose a child to locate the letter on the banner or in the room.*)

Birds and Insects

Supplies
- photographs of a variety of birds
- photographs of a variety of insects

Directions
Play "Is it a bird, or is it an insect?" Prior to playing the game, engage the children in a discussion of the differences between birds and insects: two legs/six legs, feathers/no feathers, and so on. Hold up one photograph at a time and ask if it's a bird or an insect. If your group is small enough, engage the children in a discussion about whether they have seen any of these birds or insects before.

Categories

Supplies
- category names printed on paper
- small box or bag

Directions
Place all the category names into a bag or a box and tell the children that you are going to ask them to think very hard. Tell them that you will pull out a *category*, which is a wonderful word for "a group of things," and that when you announce the category, you want them to name things that belong in that category.

Category Names

- Colors
- Kinds of Pets
- Pieces of Clothing
- Animals

- Fun Places to Visit
- Kinds of Weather
- Modes of Transportation
- Family Members
- Community Helpers

Color Cards

Supplies

- color cards—all uppercase names of colors printed in color (for example, "GREEN" printed or written in green)

Directions

Explain to the children that you are tired of reading and now it is their turn! Tell them you are going to show them some color names and you want them to read the names out loud for you. (Children catch on very quickly that the name is written in the color.) After they have correctly named the color, read each letter aloud and then say the color name again. Celebrate the fact that the children are such good "readers."

Emotion Vocabulary

Giving names to emotions helps young children manage them in a healthy way. In this game, you begin with more common words for emotions: happy, sad, angry, scared, and so on. Engage the children in a discussion about what these emotions look like. When a person is happy, how does her face look? What about when she is sad? Continue asking similar questions about other emotions. Once you have moved through the familiar emotions, talk about less familiar emotions—frustrated, surprised, tense, and so forth. What do those feelings look like? Recall a time you felt frustrated or surprised or tense and tell the children what made you feel that way and, perhaps, what you did to mediate it.

Another approach is to talk about words that describe a particular emotion. Choosing one emotion at a session, discuss other words that mean the same thing. Talk about the different levels of emotions—"If happy looks like this (*show happy face*), what do you think joyous looks like?" Act out the levels of emotions with your whole body. You might even get the children and families up on their feet to act out emotions together.

Emotion Words

- Happy—glad, cheerful, joyous, merry, jolly, blissful, chipper
- Sad—forlorn, unhappy, depressed, heartbroken, mournful, weepy, sorrowful
- Angry—mad, furious, enraged, cross, ticked, miffed, incensed
- Scared—frightened, terrified, afraid, horrified, petrified, alarmed, panicked
- Tired—exhausted, beat, sleepy, weary, drained, bushed, fatigued
- Surprised—shocked, stunned, caught unawares, astounded, flabbergasted, stupefied, dumbstruck

Flashlight Vocabulary

Supplies
- photographs of interesting items hung about the storytime room
- flashlight
- tape

Directions

Before storytime begins, tape the photographs around the room. At the designated time in the storytime, turn the lights down or off, turn on the flashlight, and shine its light on one photo at a time. Encourage the children to identify the item and describe it. Ask open-ended questions to build vocabulary.

Letter/Number Game

Supplies
- cards (index cards or laminated card-sized paper) of numbers 1–20 and some higher numbers
- cards of the individual letters of the alphabet (all uppercase letters for younger storytime groups; mixed uppercase and lowercase letters for older groups)

Directions

Mix the number and letter cards together and hold them face down in your lap. Flip them up one at a time and ask, "Letter or number?" If the children are very adept at recognition, speed up the flipping. If the children are struggling, slow down and spend time talking about each number or letter. This game is intended to be fun, not stressful!

Lowercase/Uppercase Matching Game

Supplies
- cards or papers printed with individual uppercase letters
- cards or papers printed with individual lowercase letters
- tape

Directions

Tape the uppercase letters on the walls of your storytime room. Gather the children in the center of the room and give them each a lowercase letter. Tell the children (and their caregivers) that you are going to play music and when the music stops, you want them to be standing with the uppercase letter that corresponds to the lowercase letter in their hands. Allow lots of music time so the children don't crash into one another. Let each child hold up and name his or her letter. Then have all the children return to the center of the room, exchange letters, and begin again. For very large groups, you may need to print multiple copies of the letters.

Microphone Game

Supplies
- fake/toy microphone

Directions

Make a "microphone" from a black dowel and a Styrofoam ball painted with silver glitter. (Or purchase one from a costume shop or online.) The microphone can be used in any storytime to encourage children to speak. For example, if the storytime is about food, you might speak into the "microphone" and talk about your favorite food—what it tastes like, what it smells like, where you first ate it, why it's your favorite, and so on. Then ask the children if anyone would like to talk about his or her favorite food. Hold the microphone in front of the volunteer and let the child describe his or her favorite food. Move around the storytime room and give all willing children a chance to share. The microphone can be used for many themes, and children *love* it!

Moon and Sun Game

Supplies
- drawing or clip art of a moon
- drawing or clip art of a sun

Directions

Hold up the sun and ask the children what they like to do when the sun is shining (for example, play, jump, twirl, dance, etc.). Then hold up the moon and ask them what children do when the moon is shining in the night sky (for example, sleep, snore, dream, etc.). Bring them to their feet and hold up the sun and encourage them to act out their "sun activity." Hold up the moon and have them act out their "moon activity." Alternate holding up the sun and then the moon, sometimes switching very quickly between the two. Play until the children have tired of the game.

Opposites

Supplies
- words printed on cards or small pieces of paper
- small box or bag

Directions

Tell the children that you are going to pull out a word from the bag or box and that you want them to call out a word that means the *opposite*. Ask the children if they understand what you mean by "opposite." If they don't, start with an easy example.

Here are some words to use:

- Wet/Dry
- Early/Late
- Up/Down
- In/Out
- Empty/Full
- Quiet/Loud
- Heavy/Light
- Nice/Mean
- Shiny/Dull
- Good/Bad

- High/Low
- Old/Young/New
- Day/Night
- Fast/Slow
- Happy/Sad
- Big/Little
- Apart/Together
- Front/Back
- Right/Wrong/Left
- Clean/Dirty

- Tall/Short
- Fat/Thin
- First/Last
- Many/Few
- Dark/Light
- Quick/Slow
- Thick/Thin
- Stop/Go
- Rough/Smooth
- Hard/Soft/Easy

Children often come up with "outside the box" opposites, which can make this a very enjoyable game.

Photos

Supplies
- large, easy-to-see photographs of a particular subject (for example, types of food, hats, farm animals, baby animals, sea creatures, tools, types of transportation, articles of clothing)

Directions
Using photographs in storytimes not only expands children's world knowledge but is highly entertaining as well. Our nonfiction collections feature many wonderful photos, and clip art collections can be reasonably purchased, allowing us to print out incredible photographs of a myriad of subjects. Show the photographs one at a time and begin a dialogue with the children. With larger groups, if it's possible, walk through the group and give children in all areas of the room a chance to participate. Ask questions such as: "What is this?" "Where would we find it?" "Have you ever seen this before?" Sprinkle some facts into the discussion or highlight books that contain more information.

Picture/Word

Supplies
- cards of clip art or photographs of interesting yet familiar items (for example, a car, house, dog, horse, tree, child, diaper, hot dog, pair of underpants). It's fun to add silly pictures—the humor will encourage engagement.
- cards of printed words

Directions

Holding the cards face down in your lap, flip them up one at a time and ask the children, "Is this a picture or a word?"

Picture/Word/Number

Supplies

- photographs of interesting items or objects
- numbers for each of the photographs
- names of the items or objects printed on cards or paper
- tape

Directions

Tape the photographs on the walls of the storytime room with a number beside each one. Place the object names in your lap and flip them over one at a time, reading the name aloud and running your finger across its letters. Encourage the children to look around the room for the object and call out its corresponding number.

Rhyming Bag

Supplies

- simple words printed on cards or small pieces of paper (for example, book, bake, ate, cat, bear, feet, pet, pig, pit, bite, dog, pot, boot, cow, dug, due, up)
- small box or bag

Directions

Place the words into the box or bag. Pull out one word at a time and see how many words the children can think of that rhyme with it. You may have to give examples of rhyming words depending on the children's experience with the concept of rhyming. Make sure to suggest some nonsense words that rhyme with the card words so the children and caregivers know that it's the *rhyme* that is important, not the word.

Vocabulary Photos

Supplies

- large photographs of items with interesting names (for example, chandelier, escalator, cactus, rainbow, roller coaster, harpsichord, schooner, laptop, rutabaga, poinsettia, skyscraper, glacier, comet, parachute, blizzard, cupcake, violin)

Directions

Holding the photographs face down in your lap, show them to the children one at a time and engage in a conversation about each item: "Where might we find one of these?" "Have you seen one of these before?" "What words would you use to describe this item?"

Water or Sky?

Supplies

- photographs or clip art pictures of animals, fish, and birds (for example, turtle, frog, sparrow, hawk, goldfish, shark, bat, owl, lizard, snake, dog, cat, cow, duck, person)

Directions

Place the photographs face down in your lap. Flipping them up one at a time, ask the children if the animal in the photograph walks, swims, or flies (or more than one!).

Word/Letter Game

Supplies

- cards with individual alphabet letters printed on them
- cards with words printed on them

Directions

This game is similar to the Letter/Number Game. Mix all the cards together and place them face down in your lap. Flip the cards up one at a time and encourage the children to call out if it's a *letter* or a *word*. Identify the letters and read the words together.

PART 3

Adding the Seasonings

Math

IT OFTEN FEELS AS THOUGH GROWN-UPS HAVE AN INHERENT NEED TO DIVIDE the world into *subjects*. But when it really comes down to it, the simple truth is that learning is learning. It is all connected, interwoven, and inseparable. When children play with blocks and balls, they are exploring shapes and angles, which we know to be a necessary early literacy skill. If they are engaged in child-directed play with another child or an adult, they are engaging in conversation, turn taking, experimentation, and observation. They are learning language and developing their literacy skills, but they are also developing their math, science, executive function, and world knowledge skills. It's all *learning*. So a bit of focus on developing math skills can fit seamlessly into storytimes. And when you think about it, we consistently purchase counting, shape, and pattern books for our libraries. Why not highlight them? This chapter begins with a brief overview of preschool math skills followed by suggestions for activities that can easily be initiated at storytimes. A list of appropriate and entertaining books can be found in the "Math Fun" menu in chapter 10.

Preschool Math

For preschoolers, there are essentially three main math areas on which to focus:

- Numbers and operations
- Geometry and spatial sense
- Measurement

Numbers and Operations

The skills in the numbers and operations category include counting, comparing, grouping, partitioning, and composing. Preschoolers with hands-on experiences in these skills will begin school with a strong math foundation.

When working on developing numbers and operations skills, it's important to note that we are not simply encouraging rote memorization of counting numerals, but fostering an *understanding* of number sequence. So we want children to be able to count in the proper order without omitting numbers, but we also want them to comprehend that four is *more* than three and *less* than five. We want them to comprehend what the numeral 4 actually means.

Counting

Of course, counting is a huge part of numbers and operations. Before children can move on to more challenging math concepts, they must master counting. And in order to do that, they must have a firm grasp on the three aspects of counting:

1. *Number sequence* (1, 2, 3, 4, 5, etc.)
2. *One-to-one correspondence*—1 symbolizes one of something, 5 symbolizes five of something, and so on
3. *Cardinal number*—the last number named when counting a set tells *how many* items are in that set (the quantity)

We can help children develop number sequence by giving them plenty of practice counting. We also want to count past ten whenever possible because in English, the numbers eleven through nineteen have a different pattern than other sets of ten. (If they were like twenty through twenty-nine, we would count "ten-one, ten-two, ten-three" instead of "eleven, twelve, thirteen.") And since most of the books we share at storytimes count only from one to ten (or count backward from ten to one), any practice we can offer for counting past ten will help support children's understanding of that atypical number sequence.

To encourage the grasp of one-to-one correspondence, we can provide plenty of practice in seeing how many items make up a spoken number. For example, we can place one item in front of us or on the flannelboard and say, "Here is one." Then present another object and say, "And now we have two." Once we have placed all the objects before the children or on the flannelboard and counted them, we then ask the magic question, "How many do we have?" This sort of scaffolding helps develop the concept of cardinal numbers as well as one-to-one correspondence.

Using counting words as often as possible during storytime is an easy way to help children absorb number concepts without direct instruction. For example, you might say: "I have *three* books today. Which one shall we read *first*?" "You all walked in through the *two* doors to the meeting room." "I am sitting on my *one* chair here." "I see *four* mats in the front row that are still empty." When we add these sorts of counting words into our everyday dialogue, we are bathing the children in contextual math vocabulary, thus elevating their math *and* literacy learning.

Subitizing

As mentioned in the flannelboard chapter, *subitizing* is the ability to recognize at a glance the number of objects in a set (for instance, the number of dots on the side of a die). This is an important mathematical skill and one that we can help develop at storytime by giving the children plenty of practice. We can use flannelboards or even papers with a number of items printed on them. For example, if you have just read a book about birds, you could show the children papers or large index cards with one bird, two birds, six birds, and so forth printed on them. Simply flip up the pages one at a time and ask, "How many do you see?" This is a fun game to play at storytimes and is a cinch to adapt to almost any theme.

Geometry and Spatial Sense

The exploration of shapes is a perfect beginning point for preschool geometry. And what better way to explore shapes than with a large set of blocks? A fascinating study by Dr. Dmitri Christakis and his colleagues at the University of Washington (*JAMA* and *Archives* Journals 2007) demonstrated that children whose parents engaged them in block-play every day showed not only excellent foundational math understanding but improved literacy skill development as well! Not surprising since block-play with others requires communication, expanded vocabulary (names of blocks and structures, etc.), and even storytelling when children act out a scene using the blocks. Because young children learn primarily through their senses, blocks are ideal for hands-on understanding not only of shapes but also of scientific concepts like gravity, stability, trial and error, and prediction. Adding free block-play to a storytime room is such a powerful yet simple idea. Block-play can be a wonderful transitional activity before storytime begins (or after it ends) and can also act as a reminder for parents of the importance of such play.

Measurement

To understand the concept of measurement, children must first learn the attributes of measuring (weight, length, size, nearness, etc.) and then be able to apply these attributes to actually measure things. Whenever possible, it's important to move beyond the simple big/little comparison; think about capacity, area, length, width, height, weight, distance, and so on.

Comparing

The concept of comparing is best developed in young children by manipulating real objects and using hands-on activities whenever possible. We also want to help develop the children's vocabulary around comparison—tall, short, wide, narrow, high, low, fast, slow, small, large, old, young, dark, light, open, closed, and so forth.

Math Activities

Keeping *fun* foremost in our minds when planning learning experiences for children, the following activities can be easily added to storytimes to make them more math-friendly.

Attributes
Supplies
- selected opposing attributes (for example, big/little, near/far, heavy/light, wide/narrow, long/short, dark/light)
- objects in the storytime room

Directions
Choose one set of opposing attributes on which to focus attention during a storytime (for example, big and little). If you have a small group, point to something in the classroom and ask a child if that item is big or little. Choose another item and ask a different child if that item is big or little. If you have a large group, point to an object and ask the group to decide if it is big or little.

Clap and Count
Explain to the children that you are going to clap and count together, but you're going to start not at one, but somewhere "in the middle." Clap and count starting at 8 or 3, or better yet, 11. If you do this activity often at storytime, you might let the children choose the starting number. That allows them to let you know the level of their counting skills; perhaps they are very comfortable with one through ten but struggle with eleven through twenty.

Counting Fingerplays
Before you use a counting fingerplay, tell the children, "Let's do a counting fingerplay now." This draws the children's and their caregivers' attention to the concept of counting! It's easier for preschool children to use fingerplays that count up at first and count backward at a later point. And involving their bodies adds even richer learning!

Counting Fingerplays That Count Up
- "One, Two, Buckle My Shoe"
- "1, 2, 3, 4, 5, I Caught a Fish Alive"
- "One Potato, Two Potato"
- "1 Little, 2 Little, 3 Little Snowmen" (scarecrows, sailboats, children, puppies, zebras, turtles, and the like; much-preferred versions of the old song)
- "This Old Man"

Counting Fingerplays That Count Backward
- "Five Little Monkeys Jumping on the Bed"
- "Five Little Speckled Frogs"
- "Five Little Monkeys Swinging in a Tree"
- "Five Little Ducks"

Feet
Supplies
- paper (enough for each child to have a "foot")
- scissors
- foot to copy

Directions
Cut outlines of a footprint about a foot long. Pass these out to the children and encourage them to measure the room with them. How many feet from one place to another? After measuring, show the children a ruler and talk about how long a "foot" is on the ruler. For larger items and older children, encourage them to work in pairs with two feet.

Flannelboard Counting
Supplies
- 20 identical flannelboard shapes (say, 20 green circles or identical objects cut from felt using a die-cutter if you have one)
- small box or bag

Directions
Tell the children that you are going to reach into the box or bag and pull out as many items as you can grab with one fist and that you want their help to see how many you can grab at once. Grab a handful of the shapes and then put them on the flannelboard one at a time, counting them together. (If you put them up one at a time, you are reinforcing one-to-one correspondence as well as giving the children

practice hearing the numbers spoken aloud. Plus, you are modeling the practice of estimating as well.)

Floor Shapes

Supplies

- large shapes cut out of paper or fabric
- tape
- music player and music

Directions

Tape the shapes onto the floor around the room. Tell the children that you are going to put music on and while it's playing, they may move around the room. When the music stops, everyone will walk to a shape (sharing is encouraged). Call out one shape and give the children who are standing on that shape time to describe the criteria they used to identify it. Play again, calling out a shape each time.

High and Low

Supplies

- a list of selected objects in the storytime room (for example, carpet, chairs, posters, sprinklers, lights, ceiling, and the like)

Directions

When you are ready to play this game in storytime, ask the children to point up high. Then ask them to point down low to make certain they know the difference between those two concepts. Tell them you are going to name an object in the room and you want them to call out "high" if the object is up high in the room and "low" if the object is down low in the room. Practice calling out these terms a few times before beginning to play.

Large and Small Chart

Supplies

- pairs of photographs of real-world items that are large and real-world items that are small (for example, a photograph of a mouse and a photograph of an elephant; a telephone booth and a cell phone; a dump truck and a matchbox car; a skyscraper and a dollhouse; a sheet of plywood and a wooden block; a watermelon and a grape; an adult's boot and a baby's shoe)
- posterboard

Directions

Make a chart with two columns labeled "Large" and "Small." Name items in the world or show photographs of real items and have the children decide if they should be in the "Large" column or the "Small" column. (Introducing charts to storytimes is also a fun and effective way to model the literacy practice of writing!)

Loves Me, Loves Me Not Reverse Flannelboard
Supplies
   - pieces cut from felt: center of the flower, petals, stem
   - flannelboard

Directions
Build a flower flannelboard—put the center of the flower on the board (ovule) and then add the petals one at a time, counting them as you put them up. Then remove each petal as you count backward.

Math Bag
Supplies
   - small bag
   - several different numbers of items (for example, 6 golf pencils, 12 pom-poms, 14 ping-pong balls, 21 cherries, 19 cotton balls, and the like; because it's clearest for preschool children when you focus on only one property at a time, it's best to keep all the items the same color, shape, and size)

Directions
Place one set of items into the bag. Explain to the children that you are going to count the bag's items all together. Bring the items out one at a time, set them in front of you in a line, and count together. For example, pull out one cherry and count "one"; pull out another cherry, placing it beside the first cherry so they are both clearly visible to the children, and count "two." Pull out another cherry, placing it in line with the first two cherries, and ask the children, "How many? Yes! Three!" Continue in the same fashion until the bag is empty.

Measuring
Supplies
   - piece of yarn or string about a foot long for every child (and her or his caregiver). If your storytimes are very large, you might encourage the children to work in pairs.
   - objects to measure: chairs, tabletops, table legs, windowsills, bulletin boards, mommies, feet, rugs, width of the room, and the like

Directions
Show the children a length of yarn or string and model measuring your flannelboard or yourself using the yarn or string. How many "lengths" is the width of your

flannelboard? How many lengths are you? Ask the children and their caregivers to choose an object in the room they would like to measure. Give them ideas of possible items. If you like, tell them that everyone will gather together in a few minutes to share their experiences with measuring.

Moving Shapes

Supplies

- foam or paper shapes—enough for each child to have his or her own shape
- music player and music

Directions

Pass out the shapes to each child and bring them to their feet. Play music for a while and then stop (like musical chairs). Call out a shape and encourage the children who are holding that shape to raise it up high for all to see. Encourage the children to tell you what qualities they used to identify their shape. For example, ask, "What made you decide this was a triangle? Yes! It has three straight sides." Repeat until all shapes have been identified.

Ribbon Prepositions

Supplies

- a ribbon or scarf for each child

Directions

Prepositions make wonderful vocabulary words, and because young children learn best through their senses, this game helps them *feel* the words. Hand out ribbons or scarves to every child. Tell the children that you want them to follow your directions for moving their ribbons or scarves. Give the directions one at a time and model the correct move for the children.

Wave your ribbon (scarf) *above* your head.
Move your ribbon *across* the floor.
Wave your ribbon *below* your knees.
Hold your ribbon *against* your body.
Move your ribbon all *about.*
Wave your ribbon *under* your chin.
Wave your ribbon *between* your legs.
Move your ribbon *past* your face.
Hold your ribbon *beside* your arm.
Set your ribbon *onto* your head.

Wave your ribbon *over* your head.
Set your ribbon *upon* the floor.
Place your ribbon *inside* the bag.

Shape Families

Supplies:
- many varieties of two shapes cut out of felt (for example, triangles of differing angles and sizes and rectangles of varying sizes; make both shapes all the same color to help children focus on the attribute of shape)

Directions

Place one of each shape on either side at the top of the flannelboard. Hold up shapes one at a time and ask the children which column on the flannelboard each shape belongs in. (This can be a wonderful exercise in sharing unusual triangles rather than just equilaterals and unusual rectangles, including squares.) Talk together about why the children made the decisions they did (thus emphasizing the properties of each shape).

Sundial

Supplies

object to use as a sundial (perhaps a wrapping paper tube taped to the ground or a caution cone)
masking or painter's tape

Directions

Before the storytime begins, place the tall sundial object in a sunny spot in your room or in the library. Tell the children that today they are going to measure the passage of time by measuring the movement of the object's shadow. While the children watch, tape the outlines of the object's shadow onto the floor and proceed with the storytime. When you are finished, call the children's attention to the tape and wonder about the outcome together.

If you don't have sun shining into your room, you might use a flashlight to show the children a shadow's movement. Engage the children in a discussion about the passage of time.

Weather Flannelboard

Supplies
- felt cutouts: 1 sun, 2 rainbows, 3 lightning bolts, 4 raindrops, 5 clouds
- flannelboard

Directions
Use the flannelboard to count and to talk about weather (math *and* science!).

8

Science

AS WITH MATH, ADDING SCIENTIFIC CONCEPTS TO STORYTIMES IS REALLY just a matter of being more intentional when planning. Keeping in mind that young children are already natural scientists and that they learn best through their senses, we can look at the books we have chosen for the week, ponder the scientific ideas that may be in the text or illustrations, and build an activity around them.

Young children are eager to explore and manipulate the environment around them. To encourage the scientific explorer within each child, look for ways to introduce objects—photos, shells, leaves, feathers, things preschoolers are familiar with—into storytime that will inspire questions, investigation, and discussion. Anything you introduce should be concrete rather than abstract, something within preschoolers' physical experience. For example, you might talk about the warmth of the sun on a summer day and have the children take turns moving from shadow to sunlight in the story room to test the difference in temperature. You might ask: "What is the difference between how the shadow looks and how the sunlight looks?" "What is the difference in how they feel?" "What do we know about the sun?" "How could we find out more about it?" You needn't launch into an in-depth investigation of the chemical makeup of the sun and its place in the solar system. You simply want to encourage the children to share what they know and kindle their interest in the universe. With this approach in mind, here are some activities that can be added to storytimes to enhance science learning.

Exploring the World at Storytime

Animals and Babies

Supplies
- separate photographs of animals and their babies (for example, dog/puppy, cat/kitten, horse/foal, cow/calf, sheep/lamb, goat/kid, chicken/chick, duck/duckling, goose/gosling, frog/tadpole, bear/cub, sparrow/nestling, fox/kit, kangaroo/joey

Directions
Hand out the animal baby photographs to each child (or do this activity a few times if your storytimes are very large). Hold up a photograph of an animal and ask the child who has the matching baby to bring it up to the front of the room. Talk about the animals for a moment: "What does a horse eat?" "What sounds does a chicken make?" "What names do we have for bears?"

Animals and Homes

Supplies
- separate photographs of animals and the homes in which they live (for example, birds/nests, foxes/dens, cows/barns, dogs/beds or dogs/houses, cats/cat beds, fish/bowls or fish/ponds, chickens/coops, frogs/ponds, rabbits/holes, eagles/aeries, moles/holes, ants/anthills)

Directions
This activity is similar to "Animals and Babies" but with photographs of animals and their homes. Hand out a photograph of an animal to each child. Hold up a photograph of an animal home and encourage the child who has the photograph of the animal that belongs in that home to bring his or her photograph up to you. Talk about the animal and the home in which it lives: "Where might we find this home?" "Does the animal build the home itself?" "How does it do that?"

Animals Near and Far

Supplies
- photographs or books of two different animals—one that lives near your area and one that lives in an area remote from where you live

Directions
Using the photographs or books about these animals, compare and contrast them—their fur/skin/feathers, babies, food, beds, sleeping patterns, and so on. Engage the children in a discussion about how the animals are alike and how they are different.

Animal Skins and Shells

Supplies
- pieces of real animal fur, feathers, leather, shells, and the like

Directions

Pass the objects around the room or provide an opportunity for children to explore the objects at a nature table. Encourage them to see, smell, and touch the objects. Then engage the children in a discussion about the objects: "How are they similar?" "How do they differ?" "From what animal or creature do they come?" "What do they provide that animal?"

Bees

Supplies
- photographs of bees at work
- photographs of (or the actual) fruits that require bees for pollination: kiwi, strawberry, watermelon, tangerine, tangelo, lemon, lime, lychee, apple, mango, apricot, cherry, plum, peach, boysenberry, blackberry, raspberry, elderberry, blueberry, cranberry, grape, and cantaloupe
- jar of honey

Directions

Using the photographs or fruits, engage the children in a discussion about bees. "Have you ever seen bees?" "Where were you?" "What were the bees doing?" Talk about the difference between bees and hornets. Do the children eat any of these fruits? Talk about honey and what it tastes like.

Explore Box

Supplies
- box with low sides
- assortment of natural materials: seeds, leaves, stems, moss, twigs, flowers, and the like

Directions

Fill a box with many natural materials. Place this box in a place where the children may explore it either before or after storytime. The materials can be changed to reflect different seasons.

Fruits and Veggies

Supplies
- assortment of fruits or vegetables or both
- attractive grocery sack

Directions
Tell the children that you are going to show them many different kinds of fruits and vegetables. Pull the items out of the grocery sack one at a time and engage the children in a conversation about how the various fruits and vegetables look, how they feel, how they smell, and how they taste. Pass them around for the children to handle and explore. "Have you ever tasted one of these before?" "What did you think?" "How did it taste? Sweet? Sour? Bitter?" Talk about different tastes.

Gravity

Supplies
- two objects of differing shape, size, or weight or any combination of these attributes

Directions
Stand in front of the children and hold the two objects out in front of you at the same level. Ask the children what they think will happen when you drop the objects at the same time. Will the objects float up? Will they fall down? How can we make a prediction? Drop the objects. Engage the children in a conversation about why they think the objects did what they did. If possible, pass out objects and allow the children to experiment with dropping them. Encourage the caregivers to talk with the children about what happens.

Heavy and Light

Supplies
- assorted objects of varying weight (for example, a feather, brick, marshmallow, big book, pebble, rock, scarf, metal pipe, paper cup, cast-iron pot, cork, dinner plate, empty bottle, full bottle, leaf, bowling ball, yarn, melon, balloon, barbell)

Directions
Tell the children that today you are going to explore "heavy" and "light." Pass the objects around the room and encourage everyone to handle them. After the children have investigated each object, encourage everyone to sit back down or quiet down from the sharing. Ask each child to bring an object to you and then ask the group if they think that object is heavy or light. Place the heavy objects on one side of you and the light objects on the other. If you like, record the results on a chart.

Life Cycle of a Frog

Supplies
- photographs showing the life cycle of a frog or a book about the life cycle of a frog

Directions
Show the children the photographs or the book. Engage them in a discussion about their experiences with frogs: "Have you seen frogs before?" "Where did you see them?" "What kind of environment were they in?" "What sorts of plants were around them?" "What sounds do they make?" and so on.

New Moon/Full Moon

Supplies
- photographs of the moon in different stages of waxing and waning

Directions
Show the photographs and let the children tell you what they see. Wonder about the fact that the moon looks different sometimes. Engage the children in a conversation about their observations of the moon. You needn't explain the science behind the phases of the moon. You are simply encouraging the children to share what they know or attempting to spark their interest in the night sky. You might, however, identify the full moon and the new moon for vocabulary growth.

Prisms and Light

Supplies
- prism
- flashlight

Directions
Show the prism to the children and ask them to tell you what they notice about it. Turn the flashlight on and shine it at the prism. Encourage the children to describe what they see. You might use this activity to engage the children in a conversation about rainbows: "Have you ever seen a rainbow?" "Where did you see it?" "What did it look like?" and so on.

Ramps

Supplies
- a length of cardboard or a length of timber (a wider piece will make the "experiment" easier as the objects will not fall off the side)
- two different objects (for example, a ball, a toy car, a pencil, a plastic animal, a block)

Directions

Set the cardboard or wood from a table to the floor, creating a ramp. Place the two different objects at the top of the ramp and ask the children to predict which object will roll down the ramp the fastest. Roll the objects and wonder about what happened. Do this a few times to test the results. Leave the ramps up after storytime so the children can experiment and play with them.

Rocks and Minerals

Supplies

- rocks of different textures, shapes, and sizes (for example, smooth river rocks, small pebbles, large granite stones, flat slate, quartz, gemstones, rolled and polished rocks, man-made bricks, and the like)

Directions

Pass the rocks around for the children to handle or invite them to explore the rocks around a table. Engage them in a conversation about the rocks: "Where can you find river rocks like these?" "What does slate feel like?" "How are pebbles and amethysts alike?" "How are they different?" and so on. Display some rock and mineral guides for checkout if possible.

Seashells

Supplies

- a variety of seashells

Directions

Pass the seashells around to the children. Allow plenty of time for them to look at them, handle them, smell them, and so on. Talk about the shells together: "What do they look like?" "Where might they have come from?" "Who might use shells like these?" and so on.

Seeds

Supplies

- photographs of the life cycle of a seed or a book about the life cycle of a seed

Directions

Share the photographs or book with the children. Open a package of seeds for the children to see. Sunflower or pumpkin seeds make a nice display because they are rather large. Compare the real seeds to the seeds in the photographs or book. Perhaps plant a seed in early spring in a cup or pot and check on the seed's progress every week during the spring and summer. Pass out seeds for the children to plant at home.

Shadow and Light

Supplies

- bright lamp to shine against the wall (a projector lamp works quite well)
- various objects to cast a shadow (for example, a book, ball, stuffed animal, fork, toy car, scarf, glass, stick, leaf)

Directions

If possible, dim the lights in the room and shine the lamp against a wall. Hold up the different objects one at a time so they cast a shadow on the wall. You can make this activity into a game by keeping the items a secret until they cast their shadows and having the children try to identify each object. Talk together about the properties of the objects and their shadows. You can also give the children a chance to experiment with light and shadow.

Shoes

Supplies

- a shoe or a variety of different shoes for display

Directions

Engage the children in a discussion about shoes. Encourage everyone to look at their shoes and the shoes of others. Ask such questions as these: "Why do we wear shoes?" "What do they do for us?" "What happens to them over time?" "What are they made of?" Talk about our feet: "How are our feet like those of other creatures?" "How are they different?" Share photographs of different animals' feet.

Temperature Changes

Supplies

- an ice cube
- a clear glass

Directions

Before the storytime begins, show the children the ice cube and talk together about its properties: "How big is this ice cube?" "What shape is it?" and so forth. Place the ice cube into a glass and put it out of sight. After the storytime is over, wonder about the ice cube. Encourage the children to predict what might have happened to it. Ask them about how they came to their predictions. Pull out the glass and compare the predictions with what actually happened. Talk about the results together.

Texture

Supplies
- objects with varying textures (for example, sandpaper, velvet, corduroy fabric, play dough, metal, a block of wood, plastic bubble wrap, rubber, glass, rocks, fur, Gak, and the like)

Directions
Pass the different-textured objects around for the children to handle, or place them on a table for the children to explore before the storytime begins. Hold up each object one at a time and talk with the children about its attributes: "What does it feel like?" "What makes it feel that way?" "Which objects are similar in texture?" "Which ones are different?" and so on.

Today's Weather

Supplies
- posterboard with various weather icons across the top: sun, wind, rain, clouds, snow, and the like

Directions
Before storytime, talk about the weather outside. Compare it to the last time you gathered for storytime. Ask the children which icon best represents the weather today. Place a mark or marker under that icon. Look at the chart after many sessions and discuss any patterns the children see. Use the chart to generate discussion about weather and touch on the seasons.

Wild and Domestic

Supplies
- photographs of wild animals and their domesticated cousins—for example,
  - dogs and wolves, foxes, coyotes, dingoes
  - cats and lions, tigers, leopards, jaguars, pumas
  - pigs and wild boars
  - goats and mountain goats

Directions
Share the photographs of the wild animals and their domesticated cousins. Talk about the similarities and the differences.

9

Poetry

USING BEAUTIFUL, PUBLISHED POEMS AT STORYTIMES IS AN EXCELLENT WAY to introduce children and their caregivers to the treasure trove of collections sitting on our shelves. Poignant, lovely, hilarious, adorable, thought provoking—it's all there waiting for us. The question becomes, exactly how do we incorporate poetry seamlessly or joyfully into our storytimes?

Adding Poetry to Storytimes

The following are some fun and easy ways to include poetry in storytimes.

1. Use a puppet to read a poem aloud. This might be a hand puppet who "reads" and recites the poem or a finger puppet who emerges to recite a poem and then retreats once the poem is done.
2. Choose a poem in a book, mark it with a bookmark, and hide the book somewhere in the room (sort of like a treasure hunt). When it's time for the poetry moment in storytime, ask the children if they know where the poetry book is for the week. Choose a child each week to bring the book to the front and find the poem marked for the day.
3. Write or print a poem on a piece of paper and hide the paper somewhere in the room. The children can locate the paper for you, or you may lead the "search." (You might want to keep the book from which the poem was taken near you so when the poem is read, you can highlight the book and offer it for checkout.)

4. Make flannelboard figures that help prompt the recitation of the poem.

5. Generate your own magnetic poetry by printing words on a computer, cutting them out, laminating them, and putting sticky-backed Velcro on the blank side. Preset the words around the room before storytime and let the children hunt them down and place them on the flannelboard. Then read their "poem" aloud. Though the poem will undoubtedly be non-sense, this activity is a wonderful way to play with language and explore interesting words together. This is often a hilarious crowd-pleaser!

6. Create a "poetry bag" either by making one out of fabric or by decorating a paper bag. Place one or several poems in the bag and either pull one out yourself to read or select a child to pull one out for you to read.

7. Create a poetry mailbox where you receive poems from a special friend each week. Involve your staff by letting them choose a poem, or create a special traveling character who sends poetry postcards to the children.

Pattern 9.1

8. Have poetry fish—cut out fish shapes and print poems on each one. Place them all in a fish bowl and "catch" one each week! (Download pattern 9.1 from alaeditions.org/webextras.)

9. If you have a dog puppet, paste printed poems onto dog bone shapes and have the dog pull the "bone poem" for the week from the puppet's bed or bowl. For cat puppets, paste poems onto paper mice. (Download patterns 9.2 and 9.3 from alaeditions .org/webextras.) This concept would work with almost any animal puppet. If you feel uncomfortable speaking as a puppet, you may simply use the puppet to fetch the poem for you to read aloud. If you feel comfortable speaking as a puppet, then the puppet may read the poem.

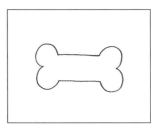

Pattern 9.2

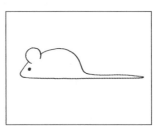

Pattern 9.3

Poetry Booklist

The following books contain a wide variety of short poems with tested appeal for young listeners.

The Arnold Lobel Book of Mother Goose, illustrated by Arnold Lobel (Knopf, 1997). Many versions of these famous rhymes are in print, but Lobel's drawings are just wonderful, and this volume is incredibly comprehensive.

The Baby's Good Morning Book by Kay Chorao (Dutton, 1986). This excellent collection provides a gentle introduction to children's poetry of the present and past.

Beast Feast by Douglas Florian (Harcourt Brace, 1994). Florian has many volumes of wonderful picture-book poetry, but this one works particularly well with storytime. It's filled with short, very funny poems about all sorts of animals. Some may be too obscure for the wee ones, but many are perfect.

Come to My Party: And Other Shape Poems by Heidi B. Roemer (Henry Holt, 2004). Excellent examples of shape poems. Preschoolers familiar with print and young, school-age kids will love these!

Custard and Company: Poems by Ogden Nash, selected by Quentin Blake (Little, Brown, 1980). Where poetry meets the witty and hilarious. Most of the poems are better suited for older children (or adults!), but there are those gems that preschoolers love and that will make adults laugh out loud.

Every Second Something Happens: Poems for the Mind and Senses, edited by Christine San Jose (Wordsong, 2009). This is an adorable collection by former *Highlights* magazine editors. It includes some simply wonderful poems by very young children.

Gracias, Thanks by Pat Mora (Lee and Low Books, 2009). A lovely book about the many things in life to be thankful for.

Here's a Little Poem: A Very First Book of Poetry, collected by Jane Yolen (Candlewick, 2007). An excellent collection of very simple poems that are perfect for preschoolers.

Higgle Wiggle Happy Rhymes by Eve Merriam (Morrow Junior Books, 1994). A collection of short, sweet rhymes and poems with adorable illustrations.

I Heard a Bluebird Sing: Children Select Their Favorite Poems by Aileen Fisher, edited by Bernice E. Cullinan (Boyds Mills Press/Wordsong, 2002). Fisher's poems are simple delights. This volume has wonderful line drawings and lots of white space as well as great poems for the very young!

Lullaby Moons and a Silver Spoon: A Book of Bedtime Songs and Rhymes, illustrated by Brooke Dyer (Little, Brown, 2003). Songs and lullabies with gorgeous illustrations. Unfortunately, the tunes to the songs are not included, but it's worth looking through.

Mamá Goose: A Latino Nursery Treasury by Alma Flor Ada (Hyperion Books for Children, 2004). A terrific bilingual collection of traditional Spanish rhymes with adorable illustrations.

Mary Middling and Other Silly Folk by Rose Fyleman (Clarion Books, 2004). Excellent picture-book collection of short, silly poems.

Moon, Have You Met My Mother? The Collected Poems of Karla Kuskin by Karla Kuskin (Laura Geringer Books, 2003). This book is chockful of poetry gems that have great appeal for young children and feature familiar subjects. Everyone should fall in love with Karla Kuskin!

The Moon Is La Luna: Silly Rhymes in English and Spanish by Jay M. Harris (Houghton Mifflin, 2007). A lovely little book with rhymes that are peppered with Spanish words.

The Neighborhood Mother Goose by Nina Crews (Greenwillow, 2004). The traditional rhymes accompanied by wonderful multicultural photographs of children in the city.

Poems to Dream Together / Poems Para Soñar Juntos by Francisco X. Alarcón (Lee and Low Books, 2005). This volume contains mostly longer poems but has a couple of gems for preschoolers in Spanish and English.

Read-Aloud Rhymes for the Very Young, selected by Jack Prelutsky (Knopf, 1986). Marc Brown illustrated this wonderful collection. There are so many great poems and rhymes here, you may have to devote a whole section of storytime to this book!

Tomie dePaola's Book of Poems, selected and illustrated by Tomie dePaola (Putnam, 1988). DePaola really understands children, and this collection of ideal poems demonstrates that.

The 20th Century Children's Poetry Treasury, edited by Jack Prelutsky, illustrated by Meilo So (Knopf, 1999). A treasury indeed.

Welcome, Baby! Baby Rhymes for Baby Times by Stephanie Calmenson (HarperCollins, 2002). This is an adorable collection of rhymes for infants and up.

Wiggle Waggle Fun: Stories and Rhymes for the Very Young by Margaret Mayo (Knopf, 2002). Features some excellent rhymes for preschoolers and some short stories to read aloud as well.

A Zooful of Animals, selected by William Cole (Houghton Mifflin, 1992). A wonderful collection of animal poems, many very short. The illustrations are wildly entertaining as well, making this a nice collection to put on display.

PART 4

Planning the Dinner Party

10

Menus

MY FAVORITE PART OF FINDING A NEW COOKBOOK IS PORING OVER THE REC-ipes, looking for gems, and dropping ingredients and adding others to suit the season and my tastes. And that is the point at which we have now arrived!

Notes for the Chef

We have examined how children grow and learn. We have tasted delicious and healthy ingredients for storytimes. We have perused math and science skills that children need to find easy success at school, and we have played with possible and palatable ways to add poetry to storytimes. Now we will look at putting them all together. The following menus are themed, but as you will notice, they are themed very broadly. Themes are not essential, but many librarians and parents find them comforting and perhaps helpful in planning. The only really important factor in the content of our storytimes is that they are jam-packed with wonderful books, stories, conversations, learning, and *fun*.

Each menu initially suggests three fiction titles. The first is a book in which the story is paramount. It is filled with interesting settings, characters, and plot elements that will engage children's minds and hearts. Such books make it very easy to pose open-ended questions and give children practice in understanding emotion, story, and event. The second title may be interactive or involve math or science in some fashion. The third title may be funny or provocative or simply short and entertaining. An appropriate informational title that may be used is also highlighted.

How many books you share at storytimes and where they fit in your own storytime plan are matters of personal preference and audience. Some librarians may use two books amid many fingerplays, stories, and games. Some may read four or five books amid only one or two other activities. These menus are designed to accommodate individual styles and tastes. Many more activities are suggested than could ever be used at one sitting. The activities and the additional fiction and informational titles included mean that a particular menu may be used two or three or more times a year. Children may recognize the fingerplays or flannelboards, but the books and activities can change.

Out-of-print titles are included in the menus. Great chefs go to great lengths to track down the perfect ingredients, and our children certainly deserve to share in beloved titles from the past. Besides, wonderful out-of-print titles come back into print every year, and some of them may still be hiding in the deep recesses of our storytime collections or on the Internet.

Each menu contains enough new and easily accessible titles to fill any storytime need. The fiction and informational suggestions are suited to most preschool audiences. However, if you come across titles that are too advanced for your children, pull out a single page to share or simply use the photographs or illustrations to enhance the learning at storytime.

The suggested fingerplays or action verses in the menus are from chapter 4 in this book. They are meant to be added to the favorite fingerplays you are currently using in your own storytimes. The menu refers to them by title, and the titles are listed alphabetically in chapter 4. If a flannelboard is listed, it may be found alphabetically by title in chapter 5. The interactive games or activities listed by title alone are described in full in chapter 6. Math activities listed by title are described in full in chapter 7, and science activities listed only by title are described in chapter 8. Suggested poems are also listed here, including potential sources, as are appropriate anonymous poems.

It is my hope that this volume becomes dog-eared and covered with notes, additions, inspirations, and splotches of chocolate.

Let's Get Cooking!

Animals

Suggested Fiction Titles

As previously mentioned, the longest story is first, followed by a wonderful interactive title, with the third title finishing the storytime on a humorous note.

> *The Three Billy Goats Gruff* by Paul Galdone (Seabury Press, 1973). A superb retelling of the folktale with folksy yet evocative illustrations.
>
> *I Spy with My Little Eye* by Edward Gibbs (Templar Books/Candlewick, 2011). The die-cut pages of this book pose questions for the children to answer about real animals. A gem.
>
> *Animals Should Definitely Not Wear Clothing* by Judi Barrett (Atheneum, 1970). A classic children's book showing many animals and why articles of clothing don't really work for them.

Suggested Informational Title

> *Who Has These Feet?* by Laura Hulbert (Henry Holt, 2011). This vibrant book shows a pair of feet across a two-page spread and then the animal to which the feet belong on the next two-page spread. Simple text and embedded interaction make this a storytime must!

Fingerplay or Action Verse

> Walking through the Forest (chapter 4)
> Zoo Who? (chapter 4)

Poem

> "The Panther" by Ogden Nash, in *Custard and Company: Poems by Ogden Nash*, selected by Quentin Blake (Little, Brown, 1980), p. 29.

Interactive Game

> Birds and Insects (chapter 6)

Math Activity

> Large and Small Chart (chapter 7)

Science Activity

Animals Near and Far (chapter 8)

Additional Fiction Titles

All God's Critters by Bill Staines (Simon and Schuster Books for Young Readers, 2009). Even though this might be seen as a religious song, Kadir Nelson's illustrations are too fabulous to go without mention. At least put it out for checkout!

Animals Aboard by Andrew Fusek Peters (Frances Lincoln, 2007). A rhythmic, rhyming song of a book featuring farm animals boarding a train.

The Baby Beebee Bird by Diane Redfield Massie (HarperCollins, 2000). Preschoolers will laugh at the frustration of the zoo animals when the new birdie prevents them from getting their sleep.

Big, Bigger, Biggest! by Nancy Coffelt (Henry Holt, 2009). This animal book compares animals by differing attributes and introduces fantastic vocabulary words.

Circus Shapes by Stuart J. Murphy (HarperCollins, 1998). This wonderful rhyming book features animals and shapes in the context of a circus performance. Great for prompting a discussion about shapes.

Dear Zoo by Rod Campbell (Little Simon, 1983). Children enjoy the many "wrong" pets sent to the little boy who is searching for the perfect pet.

Do Monkeys Tweet? by Melanie Walsh (Houghton Mifflin, 1997). Children will enjoy this simple book of silly questions.

From Head to Toe by Eric Carle (HarperCollins, 1997). This beauty from the master encourages children to move like the animals in the illustrations. Great for active storytimes.

Going to the Zoo by Tom Paxton (Morrow Junior Books, 1996). This wonderful book encourages the children to imitate all the animals at the zoo. And it can be sung!

Hug by Jez Alborough (Candlewick, 2000). Essentially one word repeated with increasing emotion makes this a fun choice for dramatic librarians!

I Am Small by Emma Dodd (Scholastic, 2010). A wee penguin enjoys being small because the love his parents feel for him is large. This is a smallish book in format, but the illustrations are vivid and nice for storytime, and children will enjoy the repeating text.

I Can Help by David Hyde Costello (Farrar, Straus and Giroux, 2010). Empathy and helping are beautifully illustrated in this circular story with bright, colorful illustrations.

If You See a Kitten by John Butler (Peachtree, 2002). Adorable illustrations pair animals with sounds that we might utter if we were to encounter them.

If You Were a Penguin by Wendell and Florence Minor (Katherine Tegen Books, 2009). Fun, rhyming text and oversized illustrations portray many aspects of penguins.

If You're Hoppy by April Pulley Sayre (Greenwillow, 2011). This retooling of the ubiquitous song has great illustrations and fun information and is a blast to sing at storytime.

Leo the Late Bloomer by Robert Kraus (Windmill Books, 1971). Leo's father worries as Leo takes his time growing up. This is a lovely book about patience and allowing children time to grow.

My Heart Is Like a Zoo by Michael Hall (Greenwillow, 2010). A variety of adjectives describe animals that are made from heart shapes. This book begs for an accompanying art activity.

The Seals on the Bus by Lenny Hort (Henry Holt, 2000). A hilarious send-up of the "Wheels on the Bus" song. This one will have everyone at storytime laughing!

Slowly, Slowly, Slowly Said the Sloth by Eric Carle (Philomel Books, 2002). A simple book that not only captures the attributes of a sloth but has wonderful vocabulary, a lesson about staying true to your nature, and Carle's signature vibrant illustrations.

Two at the Zoo by Danna Smith (Clarion Books, 2009). The counting stops at ten but the illustrations are big and bold and the rhyme will prompt children to do the counting.

When the Elephant Walks by Keiko Kasza (Putnam, 1990). A circular story in which different animals react to one another. The illustrations are simple and are surrounded by lots of white space.

Who Hops? by Katie Davis (Harcourt Brace, 1998). The built-in questions, vibrant illustrations, and silly humor make this a fun storytime book.

Whoo? Whoo? by David Carter (Little Simon, 2007). The die-cut illustrations and interactivity built into this book make it a nice choice for smaller storytimes during which everyone can see the pages clearly.

Additional Informational Titles

About books by Cathryn Sill (Peachtree, 2003). Excellent, informative text and great illustrations make these books wonderful to read all the way through at storytime. There are many opportunities for interchange as well. The series includes penguins, rodents, mammals, birds, crustaceans, reptiles, and fish. Sill also has a series on habitats.

Animal Babies in Grasslands by Jennifer Schofield (Kingfisher, 2004). An excellent book for preschool storytimes because the photographs are vivid and every other page poses a question about who the pictured animal's mother might be. Schofield also uses the same format in a book featuring animal babies in many different climes.

Animals by Peter Riley (Gareth Stevens, 2004). Though this book may offer too much information in its entirety for preschoolers, sharing one full page at storytime would work beautifully. Riley covers mammals, insects, amphibians, reptiles, birds, and other creatures.

Hair by Nicola Whittaker (Gareth Stevens, 2002). The entertaining photographs and accessible text make this a great choice for reading in its entirety at storytimes.

Just One Bite by Lola Schaefer (Chronicle Books, 2010). An oversized picture book featuring the different foods animals eat.

Life-Size Zoo: From Tiny Rodents to Gigantic Elephants, an Actual-Size Animal Encyclopedia by Teruyuki Komiya (Seven Footer Kids, 2009). This book tours the zoo, showing photographs of animals life-size. A crowd-pleaser.

Swirl by Swirl: Spirals in Nature by Joyce Sidman (Houghton Mifflin Harcourt, 2011). Gorgeous woodcuts and simple text make this an excellent storytime book with many discussion possibilities.

Tender Moments in the Wild: Animals and Their Babies (Moonstone Press, 2001). The two-page photo spreads in this sweet book will work even for large storytimes. Very simple text and the gentle subject matter make this a comforting read.

Zoo Pairs by Patricia Whitehouse (Heinemann Library, 2002). This excellent book examines the concept of pairs. The photographs of animals and the easy text make this a nice choice for storytimes.

Additional Poems

"Baby Birds" by Nicola Davies, in *Outside Your Window: A First Book of Nature* (Candlewick, 2012), p. 36.

"The Elephant" by Louis Phillips, in *A Zooful of Animals,* selected by William Cole (Houghton Mifflin, 1992), p. 18.

"Giraffes Don't Huff" by Karla Kuskin, in *Read-Aloud Rhymes for the Very Young,* edited by Jack Prelutsky (Knopf, 1986), p. 58.

"Polar Bear" by Gail Kredenser, in *Read-Aloud Rhymes for the Very Young,* edited by Jack Prelutsky (Knopf, 1986), p. 10.

"Red-Winged Blackbird" by Grace Taber Hallock, in *The 20th Century Children's Poetry Treasury,* edited by Jack Prelutsky (Knopf, 1999), p. 37.

"Wild Beasts" by Evaleen Stein, in *Read-Aloud Rhymes for the Very Young,* edited by Jack Prelutsky (Knopf, 1986), p. 16.

"Way Down South" *(Anonymous)*

Way down south where the bananas grow,
A grasshopper stepped on an elephant's toe.
The elephant said, with tears in his eyes,
"Pick on somebody your own size!"

"Little Bird" *(Mother Goose)*

Once I saw a little bird come hop, hop, hop!
And I cried, "Little bird, will you stop, stop, stop?"
I was going to the window to say, "How do you do?"
But he shook his little tail and away he flew.

Additional Science Activities

Animal Skins and Shells (chapter 8)

Baby Animal Photos—engage the children in a discussion about the animals: What are they called? Where do they live? What sounds do they make? Has anyone ever seen one? Do they look like their parents?

Bedtime, Blankets, and Night

Suggested Fiction Titles

The Mouse That Snored by Bernard Waber (Houghton Mifflin, 2000). A hilarious rhyming story of an extremely quiet family and a mouse who changes everything. There are many opportunities for acting and noisemaking (or the lack thereof) in this wonderful book.

Hush! A Thai Lullaby by Minfong Ho (Orchard Books, 1996). A lovely bedtime book with the repeating word *hush*.

Dinosaur vs. Bedtime by Bob Shea (Hyperion Books for Children, 2008). A very funny story that features a dinosaur and the universal desire to "not go to bed"—what's not to love?

Suggested Informational Title

The Book of ZZZs by Arlene Alda (Hyperion Books for Children, 2005). Large one-page photographs populate this look at the many ways animals and people sleep. Perfect for sharing with toddlers or preschoolers.

Fingerplay or Action Verse

Good Night Loves (chapter 4)

Poem: "Bed"   *(Anonymous)*

In jumping and tumbling
We spend the whole day,
'Til night, by arriving,
Has finished our play.
What then? One and all
There's no more to be said.
As we tumbled all day,
So we tumble to bed.

Flannelboard

Counting Sheep (chapter 5)

Interactive Games and Activities

Flashlight Vocabulary (chapter 6)
Moon and Sun Game (chapter 6)

Math Activity

Flannelboard Counting: Cut out about twenty moon shapes and place them
in a bag or box. Reaching your hand in, pull out a handful of the moons
and ask the children to estimate how many you hold in your hand. Place
the moons on the flannelboard and count them together. After they are
counted, discuss how the children went about making their estimations
and what factors helped them guess the number of moons.

Science Activity

New Moon/Full Moon (chapter 8)

Additional Fiction Titles

All the Pretty Little Horses: A Traditional Lullaby, illustrated by Linda Saport
(Clarion Books, 1999). Lovely, muted illustrations and a soft lullaby make
this a nice choice for a gentle storytime book.

Animals Are Sleeping by Suzanne Slade (Sylvan Dell, 2008). Muted but alluring illustrations show many animals asleep. Lovely, with a wee touch of
humor.

Bear Snores On by Karma Wilson (Margaret K. McElderry Books, 2002).
Rhyme, repetition, and a fun story make this a great choice for storytime.
Nice, large illustrations as well.

Geraldine's Blanket by Holly Keller (Greenwillow, 1984). This comforting
story follows a little pig who adapts her beloved blanket to suit everyone,
including herself.

The House in the Night by Susan Marie Swanson (Houghton Mifflin, 2008). Caldecott winner with simple text, gorgeous woodcuts, and a gentle message.

How Do Dinosaurs Say Good Night? by Jane Yolen (Scholastic, 2001). Toddlers and preschoolers will love the silly dinosaurs, the engaging illustrations, the rhyming text, and the questions posed.

Little Donkey, Close Your Eyes by Margaret Wise Brown (HarperCollins, 1995). A gently repeating phrase accompanies many animals readying for sleep. Wonderful for toddlers and young preschoolers.

May We Sleep Here Tonight? by Tan Koide (Atheneum, 1983). Preschoolers will enjoy this story about little creatures hoping to find shelter from a storm. The scary entrance of a large beast ends comfortably well.

The Napping House by Audrey Wood (Harcourt, 1984). Cumulative tale that is a popular read for both children and adults.

Siesta by Ginger Foglesong Guy (Greenwillow, 2005). A Spanish/English bilingual book about two young friends assembling everything they will need for a nap in the backyard.

Sleep, Big Bear, Sleep by Maureen Wright (Marshall Cavendish Children, 2009). The antics of the bear who mishears a message from Old Man Winter will greatly amuse the children at storytime.

So Sleepy Story by Uri Shulevitz (Farrar, Straus and Giroux, 2006). A lilting story whose illustrations will work more effectively for smaller groups. Very sleepy.

Ten in the Bed by Jane Cabrera (Holiday House, 2000). The old song is accompanied by vivid illustrations in this book you can sing.

Ten in the Den by John Butler (Peachtree, 2005). A book you can sing, with detailed and adorable illustrations.

Ten, Nine, Eight by Molly Bang (Greenwillow, 1983). This gentle counting book begins at ten and counts down to sleep.

Tuck Me In by Dean Hacohen (Candlewick, 2010). Cut pages, repetition, and very simple text make this a perfect choice for the younger storytime children.

What? Cried the Granny: An Almost Bedtime Story by Kate Lum (Dial Books for Young Readers, 1999). Granny does all sorts of outlandish yet handy things to help her grandchild get to sleep. Preschoolers find this one very amusing.

When Sheep Sleep by Laura Numeroff (Abrams Books for Young Readers, 2006). The large illustrations, repetition, and rhyme make this a nice choice for storytimes. Plus, one can make many snoring noises for added entertainment.

Additional Informational Titles

One Nighttime Sea by Deborah Lee Rose (Scholastic, 2003). Large illustrations count out many sea creatures who are awake when children are asleep.

Sleep Is for Everyone by Paul Showers (HarperCollins, 1997). Nicely illustrated, this could be read in its entirety or a few pages could be singled out to start a discussion about sleep and sleep habits.

Additional Poems

"The Dream Keeper" by Langston Hughes, in *The 20th Century Children's Poetry Treasury,* edited by Jack Prelutsky (Knopf, 1999), p. 31.

"Glass Covers Windows" by Nikki Giovanni, in *The 20th Century Children's Poetry Treasury,* edited by Jack Prelutsky (Knopf, 1999), p. 85.

"Good Night, Good Night" by Dennis Lee, in *Read-Aloud Rhymes for the Very Young,* edited by Jack Prelutsky (Knopf, 1986), p. 88.

"Night Bear" by Lee Bennett Hopkins, in *Here's a Little Poem,* collected by Jane Yolen (Candlewick, 2007), p. 88.

"Sheep" by Mike Thaler, in *A Zooful of Animals,* selected by William Cole (Houghton Mifflin, 1992), p. 67.

"The Stars Show" by Nicola Davies, in *Outside Your Window: A First Book of Nature* (Candlewick, 2012), p. 100.

"Night Light Tongue Twister"   *(Author unknown)*

You've no need to light a night-light
On a light night like tonight,
For a night-light's light is a slight light,
And tonight's a night that's light.
When a night's light, like tonight's light,
It is really not quite right
To light night-lights with their slight lights
On a light night like tonight.

Bugs

Suggested Fiction Titles

The Giant Jam Sandwich by John Vernon Lord (Houghton Mifflin, 1972). Preschoolers will enjoy this rhyming story about a town's creative way of getting rid of wasps.

I Love Bugs by Philemon Sturges (HarperCollins, 2005). Simple text, many varieties of bugs, large illustrations, rhyme, and a gentle ending make this a nice choice for storytimes.

Ten Little Caterpillars by Bill Martin Jr. (Beach Lane Books, 2011). A wonderful counting book that counts using ordinal numbers (first, second, third, and so on). Very simple with beautiful illustrations by Lois Ehlert and some wonderful science connections as well—a winner!

Suggested Informational Title

Pattern Bugs by Trudy Harris (Millbrook Press, 2001). This amusing book features math prompts, information, and many vivid bugs. The interaction is built in and so is the fun.

Fingerplay or Story

Bugs in the Yard (chapter 4)
Bugs Move (chapter 4)

Poem: Little Miss Muffet   *(Mother Goose)*

Little Miss Muffet
Sat on a Tuffet
Eating her curds and whey.
Along came a spider and sat down beside her
And frightened Miss Muffet away.

Interactive Game

Birds and Insects (chapter 6)

Math Activity

Cut out enough *L*'s, *D*'s, *F*'s, and *B*'s for all the children. Explain that the *L* stands for *ladybug*. Show a photo of a ladybug, place an *L* beside it, and place it in one corner of the room. Show a photo of a dragonfly and put it and the *D* in another corner. A firefly photo and the *F* go into the third corner, and the *B* and the butterfly photo go into the last corner. Pass out the letters to the children. Play music or clap or snap and encourage all bugs to gather in their corners. Count each corner's inhabitants.

Play music and let all the bugs mix together. Talk about each of the bugs and the children's experiences with them. Collect the letters, mix them up, and play again if everyone wishes.

Science Activity
Bees (chapter 8)

Additional Fiction Titles
Beetle Bop by Denise Fleming (Atheneum Books for Young Readers, 2002). Wonderful vocabulary, rhyme, and oversized vibrant illustrations make this a nice choice. The text is simple so there are many opportunities to engage the children in discussion and observation.

Be Nice to Spiders by Helen Graham (HarperCollins, 1967). The illustrations in this classic are rather small and detailed, but all children should hear this wonderful story read aloud at least once. And there are some great spider–science connections that might spark discussion.

Bugs for Lunch by Margery Facklam (Charlesbridge, 1999). This realistic rhyming book looks at the many creatures (including humans!) that eat bugs. The illustrations are large, attractive, and ideal for storytime, and the content will likely generate a lot of wonderful discussion!

Butterfly, Butterfly by Petr Horáček (Candlewick, 2007). Bright illustrations, the introduction of many colors and bugs, and the wonderful surprise pop-up ending will amuse and delight the children at storytime. Great for discussion as well.

The Caterpillar and the Polliwog by Jack Kent (Prentice-Hall, 1982). This classic about two creatures that grow into new creatures still reads beautifully at storytime and has repetition for participation.

Inch by Inch by Leo Lionni (Astor-Honor, 1960). A wonderful story about a worm and his clever escape from birds. And with math possibilities too!

The Itsy Bitsy Spider by Iza Trapani (Whispering Coyote Press, 1993). The short song has been lengthened into a rhyming story of a persistent spider. The illustrations are nice, and everyone can sing at least part of the song.

Ladybug, Ladybug by Ruth Brown (Dutton, 1988). A beautifully illustrated version of the old rhyme. It features some wonderful wild and domestic creatures and could easily spark discussion.

Max's ABC by Rosemary Wells (Viking, 2006). Children enjoy the bright and bold illustrations of Max trying to rid himself of ants. The large alphabet letters make this a terrific book to read through and then repeat, focusing on the letters, sounds, and story.

Old Black Fly by Jim Aylesworth (Henry Holt, 1995). A hilarious rhyming alphabet book with spot-on illustrations by Stephen Gammell. The repeating phrase makes for nice participation as well.

Spider on the Floor by Bill Russell, illustrated by True Kelley (Crown, 1993). The book is small in format, but the illustrations are oversized in relation and so wonderfully silly that they deserve to be seen. Plus, you can sing the whole thing!

Ugh! A Bug by Mary Bono (Walker, 2002). This informative title discusses many bugs and how to act around them. The cute, oversized illustrations and rhyming text make this a great choice for storytimes.

The Very Busy Spider by Eric Carle (Philomel Books, 1984). Children will enjoy the many animal sounds in the book, the growing spider web, and the repeating phrase.

The Very Hungry Caterpillar by Eric Carle (Philomel Books, 1994). Every child deserves to hear and see this classic from the master.

The Very Lazy Ladybug by Isobel Finn (Tiger Tales, 2001). Preschoolers will enjoy the antics of this ladybug as she hitches a ride on many jungle animals. The illustrations are colorful, and there is nice repetition to the story.

Additional Informational Titles

Brilliant Bees by Linda Glaser (Millbrook Press, 2003). Large illustrations and fairly simple but accurate text make this a nice choice to read aloud in the spring.

Buzz, Bee, Buzz! by Dana Meachen Rau (Marshall Cavendish Benchmark, 2008). A small book, but the photographs are still large and great for storytime. Very simple text makes this a quick read-through for younger groups.

Let's Look at Snails by Laura Hamilton Waxman (Lerner, 2010). A simple, photographic look at snails.

Additional Poems

"Bugs Never Speak" by Karla Kuskin, in *Moon, Have You Met My Mother? The Collected Poems of Karla Kuskin* (Laura Geringer Books, 2003), p. 64.

"Spiders" by Karla Kuskin, in *Moon, Have You Met My Mother? The Collected Poems of Karla Kuskin* (Laura Geringer Books, 2003), p. 58.

Cats

Suggested Fiction Titles

Fat Cat: A Danish Folktale by Margaret Read MacDonald (August House Littlefolk, 2001). MacDonald's charming retelling features memorable repetition, great vocabulary, and an appealing story.

Kitten's First Full Moon by Kevin Henkes (Greenwillow, 2004). This Caldecott winner also works beautifully as a storytime book.

What Will Fat Cat Sit On? by Jan Thomas (Harcourt, 2007). Large, cartoony illustrations and a funny, repetitive story make this a winning addition to storytimes.

Suggested Informational Title

Guess Who Purrs? by Dana Meachen Rau (Marshall Cavendish Benchmark, 2009). Children will answer the question the book poses on the first page, but the photographs are wonderful and the bilingual text makes it an interesting choice for groups with Spanish-speaking attendees.

Fingerplay or Story

My Little Kitty (chapter 4)

Poem

"*Flaco* Means Skinny" by Jay M. Harris, in *The Moon Is La Luna: Silly Rhymes in English and Spanish* (Houghton Mifflin, 2007), unp.

Flannelboard

The Rat, the Gnat, and the Fine, Fat Cat (chapter 5)

Interactive Game

Microphone (chapter 6): Describe your pet cat if you have one or an experience that you have had with a cat or cats. Passing the microphone around, or holding it in front of children who wish to contribute, encourage them to share something they know about cats. Or describe something that you *like* about cats. Ask the children to take a minute to think of something that they like about cats.

Math Activity

Print pictures of cats and tape them (or place stuffed animal cats!) around your story room. At the chosen moment in your storytime, ask the children if they noticed that there are lots of cats in the room and tell them you want their help to count them all. (Make sure there are at least twenty so the children have an opportunity to count past ten.)

Science Activity

Wild and Domestic (chapter 8): Share a book about wild cats or photographs of wild cats. Compare lions and tigers and jaguars and pumas, describing how they are alike and how they are different. Share photos of house cats and talk about the ways in which they are alike and different. Then look at similarities and differences between the wild cats and the domesticated cats.

Additional Fiction Titles

Bittle by Patricia MacLachlan (Joanna Cotler Books, 2004). A dog and a cat wonder if they will like the new baby. Preschoolers familiar with infants will find this book especially appealing.

A Cat Like That by Wendy Wahman (Henry Holt, 2011). A winner for preschool storytimes with its bright illustrations, good humor, and great information about all things cat.

Feathers for Lunch by Lois Ehlert (Harcourt Brace Jovanovich, 1990). This is a simple book for storytimes, but the large illustrations, the hungry cat, and the happy ending (for the bird!) make it quite popular.

Have You Seen My Cat? by Eric Carle (Simon and Schuster Books for Young Readers, 1987). A wonderful repeating sentence and Carle's signature cut-paper illustrations make this an excellent book for storytimes. Use it to spark discussion about the different places to which the boy travels.

I Don't Want a Cool Cat by Emma Dodd (Little, Brown, 2010). The large illustrations and the fantastic vocabulary make this a winner.

I Love Cats by Sue Stainton (Katherine Tegen Books, 2007). Repetition, interesting vocabulary, and great illustrations make this a lovely book for storytime.

Kitten from One to Ten by Mirra Ginsburg (Crown, 1980). Not only a simple counting book but a simple counting book with a nice story.

Kitty's Cuddles by Jane Cabrera (Holiday House, 2007). The large, bright illustrations, the repetition, and the many different animals make this a cuddly winner for storytime.

Millions of Cats by Wanda Gág (Coward, McCann, 1988). A classic story with a wonderful repeating phrase. Best for older preschoolers and younger, school-age children.

Mrs. McTats and Her Houseful of Cats by Alyssa Satin Capucilli (Margaret K. McElderry Books, 2001). An alphabet of cats (and one dog) makes for great fun (and learning).

So Many Cats! by Beatrice Schenk De Regniers (Clarion Books, 1985). Filled with wonderful rhyming language, this story about a family whose house fills up with cats will engage preschoolers. The pictures are small, but the story is large!

Widget by Lyn McFarland (Farrar, Straus and Giroux, 2001). A darling little dog finds his place in a house full of cats. This is a small book in format, but the story will carry the day.

Additional Informational Titles

Kittens by JoAnn Early Macken (Weekly Reader Early Learning Library, 2004). A small book, but with simple text and a full-page photograph on every other page, it will work well for smaller preschool storytimes.

Additional Poems

"At Night" by Aileen Fisher, in *Read-Aloud Rhymes for the Very Young*, edited by Jack Prelutsky (Knopf, 1986), p. 18.

"Cat Kisses" by Bobbi Katz, in *Read-Aloud Rhymes for the Very Young*, edited by Jack Prelutsky (Knopf, 1986), p. 18.

"Cats Take Naps" by Karla Kuskin, in *Moon, Have You Met My Mother? The Collected Poems of Karla Kuskin* (Laura Geringer Books, 2003), p. 19.

"The House Cat" by Annette Wynne, in *Read-Aloud Rhymes for the Very Young*, edited by Jack Prelutsky (Knopf, 1986), p. 18.

"Just Three" by William Wise, in *The 20th Century Children's Poetry Treasury*, edited by Jack Prelutsky (Knopf, 1999), p. 79.

"When a Cat Is Asleep" by Karla Kuskin, in *Moon, Have You Met My Mother? The Collected Poems of Karla Kuskin* (Laura Geringer Books, 2003), p. 12.

"Yesterday's Paper" by Mabel Watts, in *Read-Aloud Rhymes for the Very Young*, edited by Jack Prelutsky (Knopf, 1986), p. 59.

Clothing

Suggested Fiction Titles

Something from Nothing: Adapted from a Jewish Folktale by Phoebe Gilman (Scholastic, 1993). The repetition and language in this folktale make it a natural for storytime.

I Want My Hat Back by Jon Klassen (Candlewick, 2011). The clueless bear will keep the children entertained; plus, the ending is very funny.

A Hat for Minerva Louise by Janet Stoeke (Dutton Children's Books, 1994). The intrepid hen tries a variety of ways to stay warm during a snowy day. Very amusing and a possible conversation starter on what makes a good hat and what does not.

Suggested Informational Title

Clothes in Many Cultures by Heather Adamson (Capstone Press, 2007). This very simple book features full-page photographs of clothing worn for a variety of purposes.

Fingerplay or Story

Getting Dressed (chapter 4)

Poem

"Dressing Too Quickly" by Jill Townsend, in *Here's a Little Poem,* collected by Jane Yolen (Candlewick, 2007), p. 14.

Interactive Games and Activities

Print photographs of different kinds of hats and engage the children in a discussion about who uses which hat and why. (Include a silly hat photo, like the Cat in the Hat's hat or the Mad Hatter's hat.)

Microphone (chapter 6): Using the microphone, describe an article of clothing that you really love (or loved). Encourage the children to individually share favorite articles of clothing.

Math Activity

Moving Shapes (chapter 7)

Science Activity

Shoes (chapter 8)

Additional Fiction Titles

Animals Should Definitely Not Wear Clothing by Judi Barrett (Atheneum, 1970). The humor of animals wearing inappropriate clothing appeals to young children and those who are young at heart!

Froggy Gets Dressed by Jonathan London (Viking, 1992). A crowd-pleaser with a wonderful repeating exchange between Froggy and his mother.

Jesse Bear, What Will You Wear? by Nancy Carlstrom (Simon and Schuster Books for Young Readers, 1986). Jesse Bear looks at all the things he will wear in a day—clothing and other things! This rhyming book could spark some interesting discussion about things we wear besides clothes.

My Mother's Sari by Sandhya Rao (Lerner, 2011). A very simple book about a young girl's feelings about her mother's beautiful sari.

Old Hat, New Hat by Stan Berenstain (Random House, 1970). Filled with adjectives describing hats, this simple book works well as an introduction to a box of real hats for dressing up (for smaller groups).

What Color Is Your Underwear? by Sam Lloyd (Scholastic, 2004). The combination of animals and underwear guarantees a hit for storytimes.

Which Hat Is That? by Anna Grossnickle Hines (Harcourt, 2002). A name-the-hat guessing game with a lift-the-flap format.

Whose Hat? by Margaret Miller (William Morrow, 1997). The hat photographs in this book make a great guessing game for both toddlers and preschoolers.

Additional Informational Titles

Clothes by Karen Bryant-Mole (Rigby Interactive Library, 1997). Simple yet sizable photographs give a nice amount of information about clothes.

Shoes, Shoes, Shoes by Ann Morris (Lothrop, Lee and Shepard, 1995). Very simple text and photographs showing people all over the world and the shoes they wear make this a perfect book for toddlers. As a discussion starter this would work well for preschool storytimes too.

Whose Shoes? A Shoe for Every Job by Stephen R. Swinburne (Boyds Mills Press, 2010). A photographic journey through shoes and feet with interaction built in. Wonderful gender-bending photographs as well.

Additional Poem

"The Smart Lady" by Rose Fyleman, in *Mary Middling and Other Silly Folk: Nursery Rhymes and Nonsense Poems* (Clarion Books, 2004), unp.

Color

Suggested Fiction Titles

A Color of His Own by Leo Lionni (Pantheon Books, 1975). A little chameleon tries on different colors looking for one that suits him. Show photos of real chameleons to preschoolers after reading the book for connection to the real world.

Wow! Said the Owl by Tim Hopgood (Farrar, Straus and Giroux, 2009). The bright, colorful illustrations, the repeating line, and the charming story of a little owl experiencing the daytime for the first time make this a favored storytime choice.

Pete the Cat: I Love My White Shoes by Eric Litwin (Harper, 2010). It introduces color, it rhymes, you can sing it, children adore it—this one is a keeper, indeed.

Suggested Informational Title

Shades of People by Shelley Rotner (Holiday House, 2009). This wonderful book approaches the idea of color by looking at photographs of children with different skin tones. The vocabulary is wonderful too.

Fingerplay or Story

My Painting (chapter 4)

Poem

"Crayons" by Marchette Chute, in *Read-Aloud Rhymes for the Very Young*, edited by Jack Prelutsky (Knopf, 1986), p. 86.

Flannelboards

Shapes and Colors (chapter 5)
Bubbles (chapter 5)

Interactive Game

Color Cards (chapter 6)

Math Activity

Ribbon Prepositions (chapter 7)

Science Activity

Prisms and Light (chapter 8)

Additional Fiction Titles

The Artist Who Painted a Blue Horse by Eric Carle (Philomel Books, 2011). Carle's traditional painted tissue illustrations show animals in "artistic" colors. Great for a discussion starter.

Baby Bear Sees Blue by Ashley Wolff (Beach Lane Books, 2012). Though some of the colors highlighted are not all that obvious in the illustrations, the story of the little bear explorer, the oversized illustrations, the repeating text, and the rainbow at the end make this a nice choice for storytime.

Blue Chameleon by Emily Gravett (Simon and Schuster Books for Young Readers, 2011). Wonderful humor, vibrant color, and a simple story make this a great storytime book for all ages.

Brown Bear, Brown Bear, What Do You See? by Bill Martin Jr. (Henry Holt, 1992). For anyone living outside a cave, I feel no need to annotate this one.

Dog's Colorful Day: A Messy Story about Colors and Counting by Emma Dodd (Puffin Books, 2003). Preschoolers love following Dog as he gathers colors throughout the day. Makes a wonderful flannelboard too!

Duckie's Rainbow by Frances Barry (Candlewick, 2004). A very simple book with brilliant colors and a unique arched shape. Popular with the youngest but interesting to the preschoolers as the turned pages reveal the rainbow.

Freight Train by Donald Crews (Greenwillow, 1978). This simple book combines colors, train cars, and great vocabulary. A must-read for all ages.

I Spy with My Little Eye by Edward Gibbs (Templar Books/Candlewick, 2011). The large illustrations in this book are perfect for storytimes, as is the interactive question-and-answer format. Plus, it would pair very well with nonfiction books about animals.

Lemons Are Not Red by Laura Vaccaro Seeger (Roaring Brook Press, 2004). Such a creative author! This book uses cutouts to examine color. Vivid and interactive.

Little Blue and Little Yellow by Leo Lionni (McDowell, Obolensky, 1959). Lionni not only demonstrates color mixing in this adorable classic but also captures emotions in blots! Genius.

Mouse Paint by Ellen Stoll Walsh (Harcourt Brace Jovanovich, 1989). A classic story of the little mice who mix paint to make all sorts of colors.

My Crayons Talk by Patricia Hubbard (Henry Holt, 1995). A simple book about colors. Easy enough for toddlers, but if you teach preschoolers the repeating phrase, they will enjoy hearing it as well.

Patrick Paints a Picture by Saviour Pirotta (Frances Lincoln Children's Books, 2007). The color guessing and the assorted animals give this book great appeal for preschoolers.

Red Is a Dragon by Roseanne Thong (Chronicle Books, 2001). Thong's rhyming book glows with vibrant Chinese-inspired illustrations by Grace Lin.

Siesta by Ginger Foglesong Guy (Greenwillow, 2005). A Spanish/English bilingual book about two young friends assembling all the colorful items they will need for a nap in the backyard.

White Rabbit's Color Book by Alan Baker (Kingfisher Books, 1994). A cute little rabbit dunking into bowls filled with various colors illustrates the concepts of color and color mixing in a clear and attractive format.

Additional Informational Titles

Growing Colors by Bruce McMillan (Lothrop, Lee and Shepard, 1988). This book is so simple, only one word per page, but the photographs just beg for conversation. A gem for all ages.

Of Colors and Things by Tana Hoban (Mulberry Books, 1996). A wordless book with dozens of photographs of colorful items. A few pages shared with children about a particular color could help encourage interaction.

Orange Everywhere by Kristin Sterling (Lerner, 2011). This is one volume in a terrific series called Colors Everywhere. Each book features wide-ranging information on a particular color. Perfect for storytime! (In addition to orange, the series covers black, blue, brown, gray, green, pink, purple, red, silver and gold, white, and yellow.)

Vincent's Colors by Vincent van Gogh (Metropolitan Museum of Art; Chronicle Books, 2005). One sentence per page introduces many colors and many paintings by van Gogh. Wonderful as a dialogue starter.

Why Are Animals Blue? by Melissa Stewart (Enslow, 2009). This is one of a series of photography books that focus on animals of a particular color. Pages from these books could spark discussion during preschool storytimes. (In addition to blue animals, the series covers green, orange, purple, red, and yellow animals.)

Why Is Blue Dog Blue? A Tale of Colors by George Rodrigue (Stewart, Tabori and Chang, 2001). This fantastic book not only introduces an artist's ponderings about choosing colors but introduces some unusual color names as well.

Additional Poem

"Bubbles" by Carl Sandburg, in *Tomie dePaola's Book of Poems*, selected and illustrated by Tomie dePaola (Putnam, 1988), p. 21.

Dogs

Suggested Fiction Titles

Widget by Lyn McFarland (Farrar, Straus and Giroux, 2001). A little dog looks for a home where cats rule the roost. This is an amusing book with wonderful moments of suspense.

Dogs by Emily Gravett (Simon and Schuster Books for Young Readers, 2010). Many different kinds of beloved dogs are described by a narrator whose identity provides a surprise ending.

Bark, George by Jules Feiffer (HarperCollins, 1999). A mother dog tries to cure her puppy of uttering other animal noises. A hilarious book.

Suggested Informational Title

Arf! Beg! Catch! Dogs from A to Z by Henry Horenstein (Scholastic, 1999). A simple alphabet book of dogs with large and alluring photographs. Perfect for discussion!

Fingerplay or Story

Tippy-Tappy (chapter 4)

Poem

"My Puppy" by Aileen Fisher, in *Here's a Little Poem,* collected by Jane Yolen (Candlewick, 2007), p. 36.

Flannelboard

Counting Puppies (chapter 5; math activity too!)

Interactive Games and Activities

Using *Arf! Beg! Catch! Dogs from A to Z*, go through the alphabet and ask the children what they see in the photographs. Talk about the concepts and point out the letters.

Microphone (chapter 6): Describe your dog, if you have one (or a dog you wish you could have, or a friend's dog, or any dog). Encourage the children to describe their dogs. Ask some open-ended questions about dogs to keep the children talking.

Math Activity

Floor Shapes (chapter 7): The children could pretend to be dogs as they move to the music!

Science Activities

Share a dog breed book from the library. Pick out a few very different dog breeds and engage the children in a discussion about their differences (size, weight, sound of bark, fur, and the like) and their similarities (noses, growls, manners, loyalty, and so forth). Encourage the children to talk about dogs they have known or have seen.

Talk with the children about the fact that dogs are very different and that strange dogs may not always be friendly and should be treated accordingly.

Additional Fiction Titles

Bittle by Patricia MacLachlan (Joanna Cotler Books, 2004). A dog and a cat wonder if they will like the new baby. Preschoolers familiar with infants will find this book especially appealing.

Dog Loves Books by Louise Yates (Knopf, 2010). Librarians will love sharing this imaginative book about a dog who opens a bookstore. The illustrations are a bit small for large storytimes, but the story is big enough to share.

The Doghouse by Jan Thomas (Harcourt, 2008). Children will love the hilarious mystery of why the animals keep disappearing into the doghouse.

A Dog Needs a Bone by Audrey Wood (Blue Sky Press, 2007). In hilarious rhyming text a dog pleads for a treat from his mistress. This is a very funny book.

Dog's Colorful Day: A Messy Story about Colors and Counting by Emma Dodd (Puffin Books, 2003). A dog's adventures through the day leave him with spots of different colors.

The Great Gracie Chase by Cynthia Rylant (Blue Sky Press, 2001). The arrival of a painting crew throws a dog's household into disarray.

Harry the Dirty Dog by Gene Zion (Harper, 1956). A classic about a dog's dirty adventure. Every preschooler deserves to hear *Harry* read aloud and gaze at Zion's wonderful illustrations.

How Much Is That Doggy in the Window? by Iza Trapani (Gareth Stevens, 1999). The classic song in adorable book format.

I Don't Want a Posh Dog by Emma Dodd (Little, Brown, 2009). The large illustrations and the fantastic vocabulary make this a winner.

Ivan the Terrier by Peter Catalanotto (Atheneum Books for Young Readers, 2007). Even if preschoolers are unfamiliar with the traditional stories featured in this book, they will adore the antics of the mad terrier.

Let's Get a Pup, Said Kate by Bob Graham (Candlewick, 2001). The heartwarming story and the modern-looking family make this a treasure.

Mutt Dog by Stephen Michael King (Harcourt, 2005). The intimate illustrations in this book limit it to small storytime groups, but the story is too endearing to leave it off the booklist!

No, No, Jack! by Ron Hirsch (Dial Books for Young Readers, 2002). An interactive guessing game of a book.

Please, Puppy, Please by Spike Lee (Simon and Schuster Books for Young Readers, 2005). Rhythmic repeating text and the adorable oversized illustrations capture puppy love in all its wonder.

RRRalph by Lois Ehlert (Beach Lane Books, 2011). A child shows the many ways that her dog can talk. Nice, large illustrations.

Woof! Woof! by David A. Carter (Little Simon, 2006). The cutouts and built-in questions make this a nice interactive title for smaller storytimes. Plus, it's funny!

Additional Informational Titles

Don't Lick the Dog: Making Friends with Dogs by Wendy Wahman (Henry Holt, 2009). A wonderful book about dog etiquette and keeping safe around dogs that you don't know.

A Kid's Best Friend by Maya Ajmera (Shakti for Children/Charlesbridge, 2002). A tad small for large storytime groups, but the alluring multicultural photographs and the charming text make this a wonderful choice for reading at storytime or for checking out to read at home.

Once I Ate a Pie by Patricia MacLachlan (Joanna Cotler Books, 2006). Share a poem from this wonderful book.

What Puppies Teach Us: Life Lessons from Our Little Friends by Glenn Dromgoole (Willow Creek Press, 2003). Adorable photos accompany life lessons in this often hilarious book. Will be especially loved by those who frequently share animal photo e-mails!

Additional Poems

"*Flaco* Means Skinny" by Jay M. Harris, in *The Moon Is La Luna: Silly Rhymes in English and Spanish* (Houghton Mifflin, 2007), unp.

"How a Puppy Grows" by Leroy F. Jackson, in *Read-Aloud Rhymes for the Very Young*, edited by Jack Prelutsky (Knopf, 1986), p. 40.

"Just Three" by William Wise, in *The 20th Century Children's Poetry Treasury*, edited by Jack Prelutsky (Knopf, 1999), p. 79.

Emotions

Suggested Fiction Titles

Mean Soup by Betsy Everett (Harcourt Brace Jovanovich, 1992). A creative mother finds a way to help her son deal with a difficult day. This one begs to be acted out! (Anger)

Bear Feels Scared by Karma Wilson (Margaret K. McElderry Books, 2008). The tension in the story as the bear's fear mounts will captivate the children. This selection also provides a wonderful opportunity to talk about fears children may have, and it rhymes! (Fear)

Unlovable by Dan Yaccarino (Henry Holt, 2001). Alfred the dog's worries about being unlovable will strike a gentle chord in anyone who has ever felt lonely. A sweet, comforting title to share. (Loneliness)

Suggested Informational Title

The Animal in Me Is Very Plain to See by Laurie C. Tye (WestWinds Press, 2005). Nice photographs and a spare format in which emotions are described and types of animals are pictured. The visual nature of this book might help some children put names to certain feelings.

Fingerplay or Story

Feelings (chapter 4)

Poem

"Sometimes" by Jack Prelutsky, in *Read-Aloud Rhymes for the Very Young*, edited by Jack Prelutsky (Knopf, 1986), p. 80.

Flannelboard

Child's Face (chapter 5)

Interactive Game

Emotion Vocabulary (chapter 6)

Math and Science Activity

Make an emotion chart with different emotions listed across the top. Going emotion by emotion, ask the children how many have felt that emotion in the last couple of days. Count which emotions seem most common. Talk together about what the emotions look like, focusing on specific facial features. For example, when someone is happy, her mouth smiles, her eyebrows go up, her eyes sparkle. When someone is sad, his mouth droops down, his eyebrows scrunch together, and his eyes tear up.

Additional Fiction Titles

Anger

Sometimes I'm Bombaloo by Rachel Vail (Scholastic, 2002). Excellent look at the enormity of anger and how it can sometimes feel scary.

Where the Wild Things Are by Maurice Sendak (Harper and Row, 1963). Every child deserves to hear about the wild things. Let the rumpus begin!

Fear

The Gruffalo by Julia Donaldson (Dial Books for Young Readers, 1999). Children delight at the repeating refrain and the different animal snacks the mouse mentions to scare away predators. But the book could be a wonderful discussion starter about unfounded fears.

Frustration

> *"I'm Not Cute!"* by Jonathan Allen (Hyperion Books for Children, 2006). A young bird becomes frustrated by always being called "cute" no matter what he is doing or feeling.

Happiness

> *The Feel Good Book* by Todd Parr (Little, Brown, 2002). A tour through many things that might make one feel good—silly, active, sweet. There are many conversation starters in this bright book.
>
> *Mouse in Love* by Robert Kraus (Orchard Books, 2000). Simple text and wonderful pictures make this look at love a great choice for preschoolers.

Moodiness

> *The Grouchy Ladybug* by Eric Carle (HarperCollins, 1996). The "growing page" format, the repetition, and the amusing grouchy ladybug make this a nice choice. Plus, the clock on each page could lead into a learning moment about time.
>
> *Grump Groan Growl* by bell hooks (Hyperion Books for Children, 2008). The simplicity of the text, aided by the incredibly evocative illustrations, makes this an excellent example of grumpiness. This book begs for discussion and connection to the children's own experience.
>
> *Grumpy Bird* by Jeremy Tankard (Scholastic, 2007). Preschoolers will delight in the antics that ensue when a grumpy little bird takes a walk.
>
> *I Love It When You Smile* by Sam McBratney (HarperCollins, 2005). It takes some muddy silliness to finally make the little kangaroo smile.

Worry

> *Leo the Late Bloomer* by Robert Kraus (Windmill Books, 1971). Leo's father worries as Leo takes his time growing up. This is a lovely book about patience and allowing children time to grow up at their very own pace.
>
> *Llama, Llama, Red Pajama* by Ann Dewdney (Viking, 2005). Little Llama's worry at bedtime is both familiar and entertaining.
>
> *Owen* by Kevin Henkes (Greenwillow, 1993). Even though the illustrations are small, the fun language and familiar sentiment in this wonderful book make it an effective choice for storytimes.

Various

> *How Are You Peeling? Foods with Moods* by Saxton Freymann (Arthur A. Levine Books, 1999). A classic title showing many different kinds of feelings but using food items as the characters. Preschoolers really love these photographs!

I Love You Just the Way You Are by Virginia Miller (Candlewick, 1998). Little Bartholomew's grumpiness rings true, and George's loving response is spot on.

Walter Was Worried by Laura Vaccaro Seeger (Roaring Brook Press, 2005). This creative book shows many different people experiencing different emotions. Emotions are literally spelled out on their faces. A great title for letter knowledge!

Additional Informational Titles

Lots of Feelings by Shelley Rotner (Millbrook Press, 2003). Full-page photographs and sparse text make this selection accessible for all ages. Perfect for sparking conversation.

The Way I Feel by Janan Cain (Parenting Press, 2000). Nice, large illustrations and one emotion per page make this an effective book for using at preschool storytimes. A wonderful discussion starter.

Additional Poems

"It's Eleven O'Clock" by Nancy Chambers, in *Read-Aloud Rhymes for the Very Young,* edited by Jack Prelutsky (Knopf, 1986), p. 80.

"Runaway" by William Wise, in *Read-Aloud Rhymes for the Very Young,* edited by Jack Prelutsky (Knopf, 1986), p. 80.

"Someone's Face" by John Ciardi, in *Read-Aloud Rhymes for the Very Young,* edited by Jack Prelutsky (Knopf, 1986), p. 81.

Families

Suggested Fiction Titles

Oh, No, Gotta Go! by Susan Middleton Elya (Putnam, 2003). As soon as the family gets into the car, the daughter realizes that nature is calling. This is a funny, rhyming book that will entertain children and their caregivers.

Mama, Do You Love Me? by Barbara Joosse (Chronicle Books, 1991). This is a soothing book about the unconditional love of a mother.

Jazz Baby by Lisa Wheeler (Harcourt, 2007). Like a bouncing jazz riff, this book literally rolls off the tongue. Children and caregivers will be snapping and bopping along.

Suggested Informational Title

Families by Ann Morris (HarperCollins, 2000). Large photographs of families around the world with simple text make this an enjoyable read for preschool storytimes.

Fingerplay or Story

Who Is in a Family? (chapter 4)

Poem

"Growing Old" by Rose Henderson, in *Tomie dePaola's Book of Poems*, selected and illustrated by Tomie dePaola (Putnam, 1988), p. 58.

Flannelboard

Family (chapter 5): Bilingual extended family vocabulary

Interactive Games

Opposites (chapter 6)

Engage the children in a discussion about what makes a family. Talk about the ways in which families are different from one another and the ways in which they are alike.

Math Activities

Shape Families (chapter 7)

Going family by family, make large tick marks on a dry erase board or a posterboard showing how many children each family has. Count the total number by ones to see how many children are in your storytime families.

Science Activity

Engage the children in a discussion about hair color and texture, skin color, height, eye color, and other traits that family members have in common with one another. Use one of the photographic family books to highlight how people who are related by blood tend to look like one another.

Additional Fiction Titles

Families

Hush, Little Baby by Brian Pinkney (Greenwillow, 2006). The large and vibrant illustrations, plus the fact that you can sing the book, make it a wonderful choice for storytimes.

I Miss You Every Day by Simms Taback (Viking, 2007). The simple text, wonderful illustrations, and repeating line will captivate children. Plus, the story inspires letter writing and dialogue about how the mail functions. This would be a great book to use with the Storytime Mailbox activity described in the writing section of chapter 3, "Books."

Kitchen Dance by Maurice J. Manning (Clarion Books, 2008). A joyfully illustrated story of a family having a night dance in the kitchen.

Oonga Boonga by Frieda Wishinsky (Little, Brown, 1990). Children will enjoy this story about the baby who refuses to be comforted by anyone but the big brother.

Tortillas and Lullabies / Tortillas y Cancioncitas by Lynn Reiser (Greenwillow, 1998). A lovely book with a repeating verse about four generations of women in a family and how they are alike and different.

Uncle Peter's Amazing Chinese Wedding by Lenore Look (Atheneum Books for Young Readers, 2006). An amusing and authentic look at family, change, and jealousy!

Daddies

Just Like Daddy by Frank Asch (Prentice-Hall, 1981). The simple illustrations, repeating text, and amusing ending make this a popular choice for preschool storytimes.

Papa, Do You Love Me? by Barbara Joosse (Chronicle Books, 2004). Similar to *Mama, Do You Love Me?* but featuring a papa instead.

Mommies

Because You Are My Baby by Sherry North (Abrams Books for Young Readers, 2008). A mommy dreams of all the many things she would do for her baby in this fun, gender-busting book.

Full, Full, Full of Love by Trish Cooke (Candlewick, 2003). Large, loving illustrations and a comforting story make this a nice choice for storytimes.

Honey Baby Sugar Child by Alice Faye Duncan (Simon and Schuster Books for Young Readers, 2005). The gorgeous illustrations and abundant love between a mother and her child will appeal to children and caregivers alike.

I Love My Mommy by Sebastien Braun (HarperCollins, 2004). This book features many different animals and is just adorable.

If I Could: A Mother's Promise by Susan Milord (Candlewick, 2008). A very simple book about a mother raccoon showing all the ways she loves her little one.

Mother, Mother, I Want Another by Maria Polushkin Robbins (Crown, 1978). The misunderstanding between a mother and her baby at bedtime is an entertaining read for storytime.

Mothers Are Like That by Carol Carrick (Clarion Books, 2000). A beautifully illustrated book that shares the qualities of many animal mothers and features a repeating line.

On Mother's Lap by Ann Herbert Scott (Clarion Books, 1992). A little boy wonders if there is enough room on his mother's lap for him now that there is a new baby in the house.

Te Amo, Bebé, Little One by Lisa Wheeler (Little, Brown, 2004). A mother sings a repeating song to her baby as he grows in this sweet book.

Babies

Baby Knows Best by Kathy Henderson (Little, Brown, 2001). The rhyming text and the humor make this a winner for storytime.

Bouncing Babies by Michael Brownlow (Ragged Bears, 2002). Preschoolers will enjoy the large illustrations and this rhyming look at the things that babies do. (Caregivers will enjoy the joke at the end!)

Hush Little Baby: A Folk Song with Pictures by Marla Frazee (Browndeer Press, 1999). The old song, deftly and amusingly illustrated, will find new fans and spur a desire for repeated readings.

I'm a Baby, You're a Baby by Lisa Kopper (Viking, 1995). A simple book that compares human babies with baby animals and what we call them.

Lola Reads to Leo by Anna McQuinn (Charlesbridge, 2012). Children will enjoy the heartwarming story of big sister Lola reading her favorite books to her new baby brother. The adorable illustrations are sized perfectly for storytime sharing.

More, More, More Said the Baby by Vera Williams (Tupelo Books, 1990). The fun, repetitive language, and homey familiarity make this classic a necessity for sharing at storytime.

No More Kissing! by Emma Chichester Clark (Doubleday Books for Young Readers, 2002). The bright personality of the young monkey and the sweet relationship he has with his baby brother make this a nice storytime choice.

Such a Silly Baby by Steffanie and Richard Lorig (Chronicle Books, 2008). Everywhere a mother goes, her baby gets swapped out for some other creature in this silly, song-like book.

Other Family

Grandpa Loves Me! by Marianne Richmond (Marianne Richmond Studios, 2009). This loving book looks at many different grandpas and all the things they do with their grandchildren.

Tunjur! Tunjur! Tunjur! A Palestinian Folktale by Margaret Read MacDonald (Marshall Cavendish Children, 2006). The naughty little child/pot in this tale will amuse older preschoolers.

Watch Out! Big Bro's Coming! by Jez Alborough (Tundra Books, 2005). A funny book about perceptions and imaginations run wild.

Additional Informational Titles

Families by Debbie Bailey (Annick Press, 1999). This lovely book looks big, but it is divided into sections: "My Mom," "My Dad," "Brothers," "Sisters," "Grandpa," and "Grandma." Photos of many different families engaged in many different activities make this a fine book to share at least in part.

Our Grandparents: A Global Album by Maya Ajmera (Charlesbridge, 2010). Gorgeous photographs from all over the world show children and their grandparents engaging in many activities together.

Additional Poems

"Grandpa" by Berlie Doherty, in *Here's a Little Poem,* collected by Jane Yolen (Candlewick, 2007), p. 39.

"Piggy Back" by Langston Hughes, in *Here's a Little Poem,* collected by Jane Yolen (Candlewick, 2007), p. 30.

Farms

Suggested Fiction Titles

Farmer Duck by Martin Waddell (Candlewick, 1992). Children love this funny story about a duck that tires of doing all the farmer's work.

Hattie and the Fox by Mem Fox (Bradbury Press, 1986). The hen's observation of a nose, eyes, ears, and so on, and the repeated reactions of the other farm animals will easily hold the interest of preschoolers at storytime.

Tippy-Toe Chick, Go! by George Shannon (Greenwillow, 2003). The little chick who outsmarts the dog plus the vibrant illustrations will delight children in this made-to-be-read-aloud book.

Suggested Informational Title

Senses on the Farm by Shelley Rotner (Millbrook Press, 2009). The attention drawn to the senses makes this a really memorable book to use at storytime. The accompanying photographs are terrific.

Fingerplay or Story

The Farmer (chapter 4)

A Visit to the Farm (chapter 4)

Poem: "Chook, Chook"   *(Anonymous)*

> Chook, chook, chook, chook,
> Good morning, Mrs. Hen,
> How many chickens have you got?
> Madam, I've got ten.
> Four of them are yellow,
> Four of them are brown,
> And two of them are speckled red,
> The nicest in the town.

Interactive Games and Activities

Duplicate small photos of farm animals with their names typed below them. Pass out the photographs and tell the children that they are part of the library barn. When you raise your hands, the children should make their animal sound. When you lower your hands, they should quiet down.

For large groups, show photos of farm animals and have all the children make the animal sounds together.

Math Activity

Using a tape measure, show the children the approximate size of a chicken and compare that to the approximate size of a cow. Engage the children in a discussion of chickens or cows they may have seen. What did they look like? Sound like? Smell like? What other animal sizes could you approximate?

Science Activity

Bring in a hard-boiled egg for the children to handle. Engage them in a discussion about chickens and eggs. If some of the children have chickens, encourage them to describe what their chickens look like, what sounds they make, what color eggs they lay, and so on.

Additional Fiction Titles

Barnyard Banter by Denise Fleming (Henry Holt, 1994). A wonderfully simple book featuring farm animals and their sounds.

The Big Sneeze by Ruth Brown (Lothrop, Lee and Shepard, 1985). A hilarious book about the consequences around the farm when a fly causes the farmer to sneeze.

Bob by Tracey Campbell Pearson (Farrar, Straus and Giroux, 2002). The amusing story of a rooster's search for his own sound plus the large, vivid illustrations will make this a favorite at storytimes.

Cat Goes Fiddle-i-fee by Paul Galdone (Clarion Books, 1985). The old cumulative song is accompanied by Galdone's wonderful illustrations in this classic for preschoolers.

Click, Clack, Moo: Cows That Type by Doreen Cronin (Simon and Schuster Books for Young Readers, 2000). This very funny book may be a bit over the preschooler's heads, but adding a demonstration of using a typewriter or putting one out for experimentation after storytime could be a very popular activity.

Cock-a-Doodle-Doo: A Farmyard Counting Book by Steve Lavis (Lodestar Books/Dutton, 1997). A simple counting book with lots of opportunities for barnyard animal noises.

Cock-a-Doodle-Moo by Bernard Most (Harcourt Brace, 1996). The hilarious mix-up of animal sounds in this book keeps the children laughing. And it's *very* fun to read aloud!

Duck on a Bike by David Shannon (Blue Sky Press, 2002). Children will enjoy Duck's daring and the absurdity of all the animals on bikes. Large illustrations and great humor.

First the Egg by Laura Vaccaro Seeger (Roaring Brook Press, 2007). Use this book to talk about the concept *first . . . and then . . . and then.* Relate it to an activity or event for the day (for example, "*First* we sing a welcome song *and then* we read a book *and then . . .*") and let the children fill in the blanks. This is a great activity for developing vocabulary and narrative skills as well as early math skills.

A Hat for Minerva Louise by Janet Stoeke (Dutton Children's Books, 1994). This classic about a somewhat clueless hen has many dialogic reading prompts embedded in the story.

Hello, Day! by Anita Lobel (Greenwillow, 2008). Beautiful illustrations introduce the animals on the farm. This is a great book for those who enjoy making animal sounds.

Hurry! Hurry! by Eve Bunting (Harcourt, 2007). This very simple book introduces some excellent vocabulary as well as many farm animals. The loving ending makes this a nice book for young listeners.

Los Pollitos Dicen / The Baby Chicks Sing by Nancy Abraham Hall (Little, Brown, 1994). Choose one of the singing rhymes to share from this wonderful book.

Mary Had a Little Lamb by Sarah Hale, illustrated by Tomie dePaola (Holiday House, 1984). The adorable illustrations make this a nice choice for sharing.

One Red Rooster by Kathleen Sullivan Carroll (Houghton Mifflin, 1992). It counts, it rhymes, it has lovely illustrations—this book has something for everyone.

One Windy Wednesday by Phyllis Root (Candlewick, 1996). This book's small format might make it challenging for large groups, but the amusing story has too much child appeal to pass up!

The Piggy in the Puddle by Charlotte Pomerantz (Macmillan, 1974). One of the most challenging and hilarious books to read aloud! If only it would be reissued in a larger format for storytimes. A favorite!

Rosie's Walk by Pat Hutchins (Simon and Schuster Books for Young Readers, 1968). A classic about a busy hen and an unlucky fox.

Silly Little Goose by Nancy Tafuri (Scholastic, 2001). Wonderful, large illustrations and a repeating phrase make this a nice choice for a farm storytime.

Summer Sun Risin' by W. Nikola-Lisa (Lee and Low Books, 2002). Rhyming poems on each page follow a young farm boy from dawn to night on a hot summer day.

Ten Little Mice by Joyce Dunbar (Harcourt Brace Jovanovich, 1990). The vividness of the illustrations might inspire a nice discussion about mice in the wild and on a farm. Plus, it contains counting backwards from ten.

Who Took the Farmer's Hat? by Joan L. Nodset (Harper and Row, 1963). This classic story of the farmer questioning the many animals about the whereabouts of his favorite hat is small in format but large in appeal.

Who Wakes Rooster? by Clare Hodgson Meeker (Simon and Schuster Books for Young Readers, 1996). All ages will enjoy the simple illustrations and the mystery behind everyone sleeping late on the farm.

Additional Informational Titles

Farms ABC: A Counting Book by B. A. Hoena (Capstone Press, 2005). Full-page photographs star in this comprehensive look at farms.

My First Farm Book, edited by Shaila Awan (Dorling Kindersley, 2000). Each double-page spread features photographs of various aspects of farm life. Ideal for lap reading, but it could work at storytimes piecemeal.

Additional Poems

"Cow" by Karla Kuskin, in *Moon, Have You Met My Mother? The Collected Poems of Karla Kuskin* (Laura Geringer Books, 2003), p. 102.

"The Cow" by Ogden Nash, in *Custard and Company: Poems by Ogden Nash,* selected by Quentin Blake (Little, Brown, 1980), p. 72.

"Hen's Song" by Rose Fyleman, in *Mary Middling and Other Silly Folk: Nursery Rhymes and Nonsense Poems* (Clarion Books, 2004), unp.

"Rabbit" by Rose Fyleman, in *Mary Middling and Other Silly Folk: Nursery Rhymes and Nonsense Poems* (Clarion Books, 2004), unp.

Math Fun

Suggested Fiction Titles

Jim and the Beanstalk by Raymond Briggs (Putnam and Grosset, 1997). A hilarious story about a needy giant. It's a longer story, but the humor will captivate the audience, and the possibility of measurement activities following the reading helps make this an excellent choice.

My Heart Is Like a Zoo by Michael Hall (Greenwillow, 2010). A variety of adjectives describe animals that are made from heart shapes. This book begs for an accompanying art activity.

Ten Black Dots by Donald Crews (Greenwillow, 1986). Probably the best beginning counting book one could find. And with terrific dot art extension possibilities as well.

Suggested Informational Title

Pattern Fish by Trudy Harris (Millbrook Press, 2000). This wonderfully fun book is ideal for storytimes. The pattern is established on a double-page spread featuring some sort of sea creature. The children are prompted to complete the pattern when that page is turned. Hilarious illustrations.

Fingerplay or Story

Numbers Like to Fly (chapter 4)

Poem

"Counting" by Eve Merriam, in *Higgle Wiggle Happy Rhymes* (Morrow Junior Books, 1994), unp.

Flannelboards

Bubbles (chapter 5)
Shapes and Colors (chapter 5)

Interactive Game

Letter/Number Game (chapter 6)

Math Activity

High and Low (chapter 7)

Science Activity

Shadow and Light (chapter 8)

Additional Fiction Titles

Comparison

> *Big and Little* by Margaret Miller (Greenwillow, 1998). The simple, repetitive text and lack of story make this a nice choice for engaging in interaction on each page and letting the children speak.
>
> *Big, Bigger, Biggest!* by Nancy Coffelt (Henry Holt, 2009). Amazing vocabulary and bright illustrations make this a real winner.

Counting Backward

> *Ten in the Den* by John Butler (Peachtree, 2005). A book you can sing. Counts backward, has adorable illustrations, is great fun, and features some interesting vocabulary.

Counting Forward

> *Cat Count* by Betsy Lewin (Henry Holt, 2003). This funny counting book plays with counting more than most. Not only will preschoolers love the cat antics but the vocabulary is fantastic!
>
> *Count!* by Denise Fleming (Henry Holt, 1992). A good beginning counting book because you see the number of items as you say the numbers out loud.
>
> *Counting Crocodiles* by Judy Sierra (Harcourt Brace, 1997). Contains counting practice, but features a wonderful rhyming story about a tricky monkey as well.
>
> *Counting on Calico* by Phyllis Limbacher Tildes (Charlesbridge, 1995). Nice large illustrations and simple text (with additional extended cat facts for interactive possibilities). This is one of the few picture books that goes beyond ten. It counts to twenty.
>
> *Five Little Monkeys Jumping on the Bed* by Ellen Christelow (Clarion Books, 1989). This song counts backward from five, children love singing and jumping along, and that is what we affectionately call *playing with numbers*.
>
> *How Many Snails: A Counting Book* by Paul Giganti (Greenwillow, 1988). Choose a page or two to share from this wonderful sorting and counting book.
>
> *Kitten from One to Ten* by Mirra Ginsburg (Crown, 1980). Another very simple counting book and a very cute story too.
>
> *Let's Count Critters 1–20* by Caolan Madden (Children's Press, 2007). This book may be too small to share effectively at many storytimes, but put it out for checkout, because it counts past ten and the layout is very "math correct"—it features each numeral and a visual of how many objects that numeral represents.

Mouse Count by Ellen Stohl Walsh (Harcourt Brace Jovanovich, 1995). Simple, suspenseful, and begins at one. A classic.

One Foot, Two Feet: An EXCEPTIONal Counting Book by Peter Maloney (Putnam, 2011). This very simple, die-cut counting book starts at one (goes to a billion!) and is great for storytime.

Over in the Meadow by Ezra Jack Keats (Viking, 1999). The old Wadsworth rhyme beautifully illustrated by Keats. Perfect for preschool storytimes.

Over in the Meadow by John Langstaff (Harcourt, Brace, 1957). Another version of the old Wadsworth rhyme with intricate illustrations by Caldecott winner Feodor Rojankovsky.

Spot Can Count by Eric Hill (Putnam, 1999). This is an ideal book for beginning counters—contains simple illustrations, begins at one, and clearly shows items to count.

Ten Little Caterpillars by Bill Martin Jr. (Beach Lane Books, 2011). A wonderful counting book that counts using ordinal numbers (first, second, third, and so on). Very simple with beautiful illustrations by Lois Ehlert and some wonderful science connection possibilities as well—a winner!

10 Little Rubber Ducks by Eric Carle (HarperCollins, 2005). A counting book, but with science connections as well because it is based on the true story of a carton of rubber ducks that went overboard from a ship and scattered to many regions of the Pacific Ocean.

Ten Red Apples: A Bartholomew Bear Counting Book by Virginia Miller (Candlewick, 2002). A nice one-to-ten counting book with the apples off to the side for subitizing.

We All Went on Safari: A Counting Journey through Tanzania by Laurie Krebs (Barefoot Books, 2003). This wonderful counting book is simple and accompanied by a repeating phrase for extra fun.

Measurement

Big, Bigger, Biggest! by Nancy Coffelt (Henry Holt, 2009). A very simple book with excellent comparison examples.

Blue Sea by Robert Kalan (Greenwillow, 1979). Children love this simple book where the little fish gets away. Cut out paper fish of varying sizes for the children to sort by size after the storytime.

Inch by Inch by Leo Lionni (Astor-Honor, 1960). Cut a piece of yarn or string and use it to measure items in the room the way the worm uses himself. Introduce a ruler and show the children what an inch looks like. Talk about "longer," "shorter," "taller," "wider," and so forth. Outline and cut out your feet and the children's feet and use the cutouts to measure things around the room. (How many "feet" is this object?)

Order

    First the Egg by Laura Vaccaro Seeger (Roaring Brook Press, 2007). Use this book to talk about the concept *first . . . and then . . . and then*. Relate the book to an activity or event for the day (for example, "*First* we sing a welcome song *and then* we read a book *and then* . . .") and let the children fill in the blanks. This is a great activity for developing vocabulary and narrative skills as well as early math skills.

Patterns

    Fun with Patterns by Peter Patilla (Millbrook Press, 1998). Use the introduction in this book to begin a discussion of patterns.

    Gray Rabbit's Odd One Out by Alan Baker (Kingfisher, 1995). Rabbit (and the readers!) must find the odd item on each page. This interactive title is cute, vibrant, and filled with learning.

    Hide and Snake by Keith Baker (Harcourt Brace Jovanovich, 1991). This very simple book has many opportunities for interaction as children look for the hiding snake on each page. It also offers an opportunity to talk about patterns.

Shapes

    Brown Rabbit's Shape Book by Alan Baker (Kingfisher Books, 1994). This clever yet simple book looks at many shapes, but also features the science of air going out of balloons! Fun!

    Changes, Changes by Pat Hutchins (Macmillan, 1971). As children watch the block characters make, dismantle, and remake their world in this wonderful wordless book, they might very well beg for a set of blocks for play after the storytime.

    Circus Shapes by Stuart J. Murphy (HarperCollins, 1998). This wonderful rhyming book features animals and shapes in the context of a circus performance. Great for prompting a discussion about shapes.

    Color Farm by Lois Ehlert (Lippincott, 1990). The clarity of the shapes as each page is turned makes this a wonderful choice for storytimes. And the animals are creative, amusing, and colorful.

    Round Is a Mooncake by Roseanne Thong (Chronicle Books, 2000). Basic shapes are introduced in this vivid book. Grace Lin provides gorgeous illustrations featuring traditional Chinese items.

    Sea Shapes by Suse MacDonald (Harcourt Brace, 1994). Each page begins with a shape and then grows frame by frame into a seascape. Perfect for storytime—nice, large, colorful illustrations.

    Shape Capers by Catheryn Falwell (Greenwillow, 2007). Children will enjoy this rhythmic story about shapes.

The Shape of Things by Dayle Ann Dodds (Candlewick, 1994). The very simple format and the clarity of the shapes make this a great choice for storytimes where younger children are present.

Shapes and Patterns by Eyelike Books (Play Bac, 2007). Large photographs cover a two-page spread demonstrating a wide variety of shapes and patterns. A single page from this book is ideal for demonstrating a specific shape or pattern concept.

Ship Shapes by Stella Blackstone (Barefoot Books, 2006). The vibrant quilted illustrations and the built-in interaction make this an excellent choice for storytime.

Sorting

Sorting at the Ocean by Jennifer Rozines Roy (Marshall Cavendish Benchmark, 2006). Use this book to introduce the concept of sets.

Supplementary Titles

Hide and Seek by Janet Wong (Harcourt, 2005). The counting in this book is secondary to the poetry of the words, but children will enjoy the concept of seeking a place to hide while someone counts to ten.

Look! Look! Look! by Nancy Elizabeth Wallace (Marshall Cavendish, 2006). As the mice examine the different aspects of a postcard that arrives for the humans in their home, they cover quite a few mathematical concepts. This book inspires many art and writing activities!

Mother Goose: Numbers on the Loose by Leo and Diane Dillon (Harcourt, 2007). A fun book filled with Mother Goose rhymes that contain numbers or counting.

Mouse Views: What the Class Pet Saw by Bruce McMillan (Holiday House, 1993). Vivid photographs of classroom items in tight close-up make this a perfect book for eliciting interaction.

26 Letters and 99 Cents by Tana Hoban (Greenwillow, 1987). This is a great photographic book about letters and coins and counting.

Additional Informational Titles

The Icky Bug Counting Book by Jerry Pallotta (Charlesbridge, 1992). This wonderful book begins with zero and counts up to twenty-six. If the information about real insects is too long for your storytime, simply use the illustrations to generate conversation about the children's life experiences with the different bugs.

One Nighttime Sea by Deborah Lee Rose (Scholastic, 2003). Large illustrations count many sea creatures that are awake when children are asleep.

Zoo Pairs by Patricia Whitehouse (Heinemann Library, 2002). An excellent book that examines the concept of pairs. The photographs of animals and the easy text make this a nice choice for preschool storytimes.

Additional Poem
"1, 2, 3" in *Welcome, Baby! Baby Rhymes for Baby Times* by Stephanie Calmenson (HarperCollins, 2002), p. 49.

Me!

Suggested Fiction Titles
Children Make Terrible Pets by Peter Brown (Little, Brown, 2010). Amusing illustrations and a tongue-in-cheek story make this an entertaining choice for storytime.

Someone Bigger by Jonathan Emmett (Clarion Books, 2004). Great illustrations and rhyming text, plus the fact that the small child solves the problem, make this a favorite.

Jazz Baby by Carole Boston Weatherford (Lee and Low Books, 2002). This riffing, rhyming, romp of a book will delight preschoolers and get all toes tapping. It is small in format, but the illustrations are large enough for many storytime groups.

Suggested Informational Title
We Are All Alike . . . We Are All Different by the Cheltenham Elementary School Kindergartners (Scholastic, 1991). This wonderfully interactive book of photographs and illustrations looks at the many ways we are alike and different.

Fingerplay or Story
Action Words (chapter 4)

Poem: "Something About Me"   *(Anonymous)*
There's something about me
That I'm knowing,
There's something about me
That isn't showing,
I'm growing!

Flannelboard

Child's Face (chapter 5)

Interactive Games

Ribbon Prepositions (chapter 7)

Microphone (chapter 6): Using the microphone, say a couple of things about your favorite food or an activity that you really enjoy. Encourage the children to share something about themselves.

Math Activities

Feet (chapter 7)

Hand out pieces of string or yarn and have the children work in pairs to measure each other's height.

Science Activity

Fruits and Veggies (chapter 8)

Additional Fiction Titles

A-Tisket A-Tasket by Ella Fitzgerald (Philomel Books, 2003). The old rhyme gets a facelift through Ella's jazzy lyrics and the vibrant, multicultural illustrations.

Bein' with You This Way by W. Nikola-Lisa (Lee and Low Books, 1994). This wonderful book with impressionistic illustrations looks at the different colors and appearances of people.

Can You Guess? by Margaret Miller (Greenwillow, 1993). The fun photographs and the very interactive format of posing questions and soliciting answers make this a winner for storytimes.

Dance with Me by Charles R. Smith Jr. (Candlewick, 2008). Young children will want to jump to their feet when you share this joyful title.

Dancing Feet by Lindsay Craig (Knopf, 2010). Even though the book is a bit on the small side, the repetition, rhyme, and adorable illustrations will hold great appeal for children.

Fiesta by Ginger Foglesong Guy (Greenwillow, 1996). Children get ready for a celebration in this simple picture book sprinkled with words in Spanish.

The Growing Story by Ruth Krauss (HarperCollins, 2000). Helen Oxenbury's wonderful illustrations bring this old story to life. A bit longer than many other storytime books, but well worth sharing and then talking together about growing.

Honey, I Love by Eloise Greenfield (HarperCollins, 2003). A poetic yet simple look at all the things that a young girl loves. Vivid illustrations will hold appeal for preschoolers and young, school-age children.

How Do You Wokka-Wokka? by Elizabeth Bluemle (Candlewick, 2009). Filled with rhythmic language, this simple book makes a fun addition to preschool storytimes.

I Ain't Gonna Paint No More by Karen Beaumont (Harcourt, 2005). Not only does this book have a repeating line for audience participation, but it also is filled with rhyming completion prompts!

If You're Happy and You Know It by Anna McQuinn (Barefoot Books, 2009). Wonderfully illustrated version of the song with many different movement prompts for a wiggling storytime!

If You're Happy and You Know It by Jane Cabrera (Holiday House, 2005). The large and vibrant illustrations stand out in this version of the popular song.

I'm a Jolly Farmer by Julie Lacome (Candlewick, 1994). A little girl imagines becoming different people, real and fictional.

A Letter to Amy by Ezra Jack Keats (Harper and Row, 1968). This classic book features an alluring story and wonderful illustrations. It also could serve as an excellent springboard for a writing activity, a discussion about friends and feelings, or both.

My Name Is Elizabeth by Annika Dunklee (Kids Can Press, 2011). The young girl's demands that people address her by her full name and not a nickname make this a funny and familiar story.

No, David! by David Shannon (Blue Sky Press, 1998). The simple text and familiar situations plus the oversize and evocative illustrations will make this a popular book at storytimes.

These Hands by Hope Lynn Price (Hyperion Books for Children/Jump at the Sun, 1999). A simple rhyming book about the many things that hands can do. Large, lovely illustrations are perfect for storytime.

Where Does It Go? by Margaret Miller (Greenwillow, 1992). The silliness of the photographs in this book will hold great appeal and perhaps spark discussion.

Whoever You Are by Mem Fox (Harcourt Brace, 1997). Excellent storytime book with colorful multicultural illustrations and a simple rhyme with a unifying theme.

Additional Informational Titles

Guess Whose Shadow? by Stephen R. Swinburne (Boyds Mills Press, 1999). Children will love the photographs of all sorts of shadows and the shadow guessing game in the middle of the book. This is a perfect nonfiction title to read all the way through at storytime.

My Five Senses by Margaret Miller (Simon and Schuster Books for Young Readers, 1994). Very simple text, wonderful photographs, and lots of possibilities for interaction make this an ideal storytime book.

To Be a Kid by Maya Ajmera (Charlesbridge, 1999). The large photographs of children all over the world doing what kids do, plus the simple text, make this a book perfect for reading at storytimes. Each page could spark interesting interaction.

What Is Touch? by Jennifer Boothroyd (Lerner, 2010). Excellent photographs and simple text help fuel the discussion examining our sense of touch. (This is part of a wonderful series by Jennifer Boothroyd called Your Amazing Senses.)

Additional Poems

"Big" by Dorothy Aldis, in *Read-Aloud Rhymes for the Very Young,* edited by Jack Prelutsky (Knopf, 1986), p. 28.

"Halfway Down" by A. A. Milne, in *Here's a Little Poem,* collected by Jane Yolen (Candlewick, 2007), p. 16.

"I Am Rose" by Gertrude Stein, in *The Baby's Good Morning Book* by Kay Chorao (Dutton, 1986), p. 54.

"Look" by Charlotte Zolotow, in *Read-Aloud Rhymes for the Very Young,* edited by Jack Prelutsky (Knopf, 1986), p. 25.

"Singing-Time" by Rose Fyleman, in *Read-Aloud Rhymes for the Very Young,* edited by Jack Prelutsky (Knopf, 1986), p. 3.

"Some Things Don't Make Any Sense at All" by Judith Viorst, in *Tomie dePaola's Book of Poems,* selected and illustrated by Tomie dePaola (Putnam, 1988), p. 53.

Potpourri

Suggested Fiction Titles

The Pigs' Picnic by Keiko Kasza (Putnam, 1988). Children enjoy the outlandish lengths to which Mr. Pig goes to impress his lady friend.

Trashy Town by Andrea Zimmerman (HarperCollins, 1999). An adorable and accessible story with a wonderful repetitive chant.

Can You Make a Scary Face? by Jan Thomas (Beach Lane Books, 2009). This book has it all—simple text, bold illustrations, embedded movement prompts, and a large dose of hilarity. Highly interactive!

Suggested Informational Title

Spikey, Slimy, Smooth: What Is Texture? by Jane Brocket (Putnam and Grosset, 1997). This book features large, evocative photographs of many items of differing textures. The embedded questions make this a wonderful interactive read for storytime.

Fingerplay or Story

Grocery Cart (chapter 4)

Poem

"Twinkle, Twinkle" by Lewis Carroll, in *Read-Aloud Rhymes for the Very Young,* edited by Jack Prelutsky (Knopf, 1986), p. 46.

Interactive Game

Categories (chapter 6)

Math Activity

Clap and Count (chapter 7)

Science Activity

Gravity (chapter 8)

Additional Fiction Titles

Bear's Picture by Daniel Pinkwater (Houghton Mifflin, 2008). A fun book to read aloud and a wonderful lesson about art. Paint on!

Bears on Chairs by Shirley Parenteau (Candlewick, 2009). This is a sweet book about solving a problem—not enough chairs for the number of bears. Could lead to some interesting discussion.

Black, White, Day, Night by Laura Vaccaro Seeger (Roaring Brook Press, 2006). This simple concept book is great for initiating conversations and making connections to the children's lives.

Book! Book! Book! by Deborah Bruss (Arthur A. Levine Books, 2001). A picture-book version of the old joke about a chicken going to the library. (Grown-ups at storytime will love this one!)

Dance Away by George Shannon (Greenwillow, 1982). The repeating refrain in this book is a set of dance steps. The children might enjoy dancing along with this book.

Drummer Hoff by Barbara Emberley (Prentice-Hall, 1967). The repeating line, the vivid illustrations, and the humor of this Caldecott winner make it a nice choice for storytimes.

Henry Works by D. B. Johnson (Houghton Mifflin, 2004). This is a sophisticated story for many storytime groups, but it could spark interesting discussion about authors and writing.

If You're a Monster and You Know It by Rebecca Emberley (Orchard Books, 2010). A crowd-pleasing, interactive, singing update of a classic—this is such fun to share!

Jazz Baby by Carol Boston Weatherford (Lee and Low Books, 2002). An energetic rhyming book featuring many children singing and dancing. Fun!

Jim and the Beanstalk by Raymond Briggs (Putnam and Grosset, 1997). A hilarious story about a needy giant. It's a longer story, but the humor will captivate the audience, and the possibility of measurement activities following the reading helps make this an excellent choice.

Miss Mary Mack: A Hand-Clapping Rhyme by Mary Ann Hoberman (Little, Brown, 1998). The popular and silly song is accompanied by hilarious illustrations and followed by creative ideas on how to share the book with children.

No Dinner! The Story of the Old Woman and the Pumpkin by Jessica Souhami (Marshall Cavendish, 1999). This retelling of an old Asian folktale features many opportunities for repeating phrases. Plus, it's a highly entertaining story.

Please Don't Slam the Door by Dori Chaconas (Candlewick, 2010). A romping, circular story that rhymes and is funny!

Shout! Shout It Out! by Denise Fleming (Henry Holt, 2011). Bold illustrations encourage children to shout out many conceptual categories: numbers, colors, letters of the alphabet, modes of transportation, and animals.

Ten Black Dots by Donald Crews (Greenwillow, 1986). A wonderful counting book and a wonderful inspiration for using black dot stickers in creative ways.

This Is the Bear by Sarah Hayes (Candlewick, 1993). A simple rhyming story about a stuffed bear that has an adventure at the dump. Discussions about beloved possessions or garbage or both could be very interesting and entertaining!

This Land Is Your Land by Woody Guthrie, illustrated by Kathy Jakobsen (Little, Brown, 1998). The detailed folk art illustrations may be too intricate for full storytime sharing, but the song can carry the book.

A Tree Is Nice by Janice May Udry (Harper, 1956). The 1957 Caldecott winner is a lovely, calm book to share with preschoolers.

Would You Rather . . . by John Burningham (Crowell, 1978). Though this may be a bit long for many storytime children, the silly questions posed on each page make it a highly interactive and very entertaining book to share in part at storytimes.

Additional Informational Titles

A Cool Drink of Water by Barbara Kerley (National Geographic Society, 2002). A photographic journey portraying people around the world enjoying a cool drink of water. Gorgeous.

It's Rainy Today by Kristin Sterling (Lerner, 2010). Excellent photographs and simple sentences present all sorts of potential discussion ideas about rain. This is one in a series about different kinds of weather.

ADDITIONAL POEMS

"Ladybug"   *(Anonymous)*
> Ladybug,
> Ladybug,
> Ladybug,
> Don't fly away.
> You're good for my garden,
> Please, ladybug—stay.

"The Storm"   *(Anonymous)*
> The thunder crashed,
> The lightning flashed,
> And all the world was shaken.
> The little pig
> Curled up his tail,
> And ran to save his bacon!

This is also the menu in which to feature any poems that you love!

Seashore

Suggested Fiction Titles

Little Fish Lost by Nancy Van Laan (Atheneum Books for Young Readers, 1998). An adorable story with interesting language and lots of opportunities for children to join in on repeating phrases.

All You Need for a Beach by Alice Schertle (Silver Whistle/Harcourt, 2004). Beginning with one grain of sand, this beautifully illustrated book explores the seashore in a very entertaining way.

I'm the Biggest Thing in the Ocean by Kevin Sherry (Dial Books for Young Readers, 2007). This book not only is highly entertaining but also introduces a lot of sea creatures as well as the concepts of bigger and smaller.

Suggested Informational Title

Sea Shapes by Suse MacDonald (Harcourt Brace, 1994). Each page begins with a shape and then grows frame by frame into a seascape. The large, colorful illustrations are perfect for storytime.

Fingerplay or Story

Down at the Seaside (chapter 4)

Poem

"The Sea Is *El Mar*" by Jay M. Harris, in *The Moon Is La Luna: Silly Rhymes in English and Spanish* (Houghton Mifflin, 2007), unp.

Flannelboard

Ocean Riddles (chapter 5)

Interactive Game

Flashlight Vocabulary (chapter 6): Before the storytime starts, post photographs of different sea creatures around the room. Dim the lights, shine the flashlight on the creatures one by one, and engage the children in a discussion about each creature: "What is it?" "Where in the sea does it live?" "What does it eat?" "Have you ever seen one of these?" and so forth.

Math Activity

Place flannel, paper, or plastic fish into a box or bag. Grab a fistful of fishes and ask the children to estimate how many fish you are holding. Count them one by one together out loud.

Science Activities

Bring in seashells, sea stars, and the like for the children to examine and describe.

Bring in a sample of freshwater and salt water for comparing and contrasting.

Additional Fiction Titles

Beach Day by Karen Roosa (Greenwillow, 1990). Fun, rhyming text accompanies cute illustrations of families enjoying the seaside.

A Beach Day by Douglas Florian (Greenwillow, 1990). The simplicity of the text (just one or two words per page) makes this a simple choice for preschool storytimes, but the illustrations are wonderful and most pages call for interaction or discussion or both.

Beach Party! by Harriet Ziefert (Blue Apple Books, 2005). This simple book shows how different beach creatures move. It would be ideal for a storytime in which everyone likes to move.

Bebé Goes to the Beach by Susan Middleton Elya (Harcourt, 2008). Bebé returns in a romping trip to the beach. Fun!

Blue Sea by Robert Kalan (Greenwillow, 1979). Children love the fish chasing and fish trapping in this simple book about life in the ocean.

The Deep Blue Sea by Audrey Wood (Blue Sky Press, 2005). A wonderful cumulative story about the sea and colors. Children can fill in the color names as you read.

Fish Eyes: A Book You Can Count On by Lois Ehlert (Harcourt Brace Jovanovich, 1990). Very simple illustrations show many colorful fish in this simple counting book that begs for decorating paper fish following the storytime.

The Hidden Forest by Jeannie Baker (Greenwillow, 2000). This fascinating story of a boy setting a fish trap will captivate children at storytime, as will the gorgeous illustrations.

Looking for Crabs by Bruce Whatley (Angus and Robertson, 1993). A family searches for crabs on the beach. The illustrations are very amusing and beg for interaction from the children.

One Lonely Sea Horse by Saxton Freymann (Arthur A. Levine Books, 2000). As in other books by Freymann, different sorts of food are used to create the characters. Children love identifying the foods, making this a very interactive read.

Ship Shapes by Stella Blackstone (Barefoot Books, 2006). The vibrant quilted illustrations and the built-in interaction make this an excellent choice for storytime.

Additional Informational Titles

Hermit Crabs by Lola M. Schaefer (Heinemann Library, 2002). Because each double-page spread begins with a question, this book just begs preschoolers to answer. The photographs are on the small side, but still wonderful.

Ocean Counting: Odd Numbers by Jerry Pallotta (Charlesbridge, 2005). The large illustrations will work nicely at storytime. Depending on the ages of your storytime attendees, you might be able to read this book all the way through, but it could also be used to highlight counting by odd numbers.

One Nighttime Sea by Deborah Lee Rose (Scholastic, 2003). Large illustrations count many sea creatures that are awake when children are asleep.

Pattern Fish by Trudy Harris (Millbrook Press, 2000). This wonderfully fun book is ideal for storytimes. The pattern is established on a double-page spread featuring some sort of sea creature. The children are prompted to complete the pattern when that page is turned. Hilarious illustrations.

Senses at the Seashore by Shelley Rotner (Millbrook Press, 2006). Large photographs, simple text, and the use of the senses to explore the beach make this an ideal choice for storytime.

Sorting at the Ocean by Jennifer Rozines Roy (Marshall Cavendish Benchmark, 2005). Excellent photographs of sets of things.

Star of the Sea: A Day in the Life of a Starfish by Janet Halfmann (Christy Ottaviano Books, 2011). This book follows a sea star as she encounters many different creatures. Large and lovely illustrations would work well at storytime.

A Walk on the Beach by Jo Waters (Raintree, 2006). A very simple book filled with photographs of objects one might find at the beach. Wonderful for reading all the way through at storytime.

Who Grows Up in the Ocean? A Book about Ocean Animals and Their Offspring by Theresa Longenecker (Picture Window Books, 2003). Probably a bit long for reading in one sitting at storytime, but the large illustrations of one sea animal per double-page spread make this a nice choice for sharing in part.

Additional Poems

"Home" by Jean Jaszi, in *Read-Aloud Rhymes for the Very Young,* edited by Jack Prelutsky (Knopf, 1986), p. 30.

"Shell Song" by Nicola Davies, in *Outside Your Window: A First Book of Nature* (Candlewick, 2012), p. 46.

"Shore" by Mary Britton Miller, in *Read-Aloud Rhymes for the Very Young,* edited by Jack Prelutsky (Knopf, 1986), 30.

Transportation

Suggested Fiction Titles

Mr. Gumpy's Motor Car by John Burningham (Macmillan, 1975). Every preschooler deserves to take a ride in Mr. Gumpy's car.

Down by the Station by Will Hillenbrand (Harcourt Brace, 1999). In this appealing version of the song, the little engine picks up baby animals from all over town (including the children) and drops them at the zoo.

The Bridge Is Up by Babs Bell (HarperCollins, 2004). The repeating line in this fun book provides great interaction. The illustrations hold appeal for children.

Suggested Informational Title

Road Builders by B. G. Hennessy (Viking, 1994). A wonderful storytime book that follows the machines and workers building a road. This would also be a great informational companion to *Goodnight, Goodnight, Construction Site*.

Fingerplay or Story

Road Trip (chapter 4)

Poem

"Taking Off" by Mary McB. Green, in *The 20th Century Children's Poetry Treasury*, edited by Jack Prelutsky (Knopf, 1999), p. 63.

Flannelboard

Transportation (chapter 5)

Interactive Games and Activities

Alphabet Hunt (chapter 6)

Show photographs of different modes of transportation and ask the children if they have ever seen them before, where they saw them, what they are used for, and so on.

Math Activity

Attributes (chapter 7)

Science Activity

Ramps (chapter 8): Use vehicles instead of balls.

Additional Fiction Titles

All Aboard: A Traveling Alphabet by Bill Mayer (Margaret K. McElderry Books, 2008). An alphabet book with only one word per page may seem an unlikely choice for storytime, but the gorgeous illustrations just beg for sharing and interaction.

Boats for Bedtime by Olga Litowinsky (Clarion Books, 1999). Vivid illustrations and sparse text make this an attractive yet simple title for storytimes.

Cars, Trucks, and Planes / Carros, camiones y aviones by Gladys Rosa-Mendoza (Me+mi, 2004). Excellent two-page-spread illustrations of different modes of transportation are featured in this bilingual board book in English and Spanish.

Chugga-Chugga Choo-Choo by Kevin Lewis (Hyperion Books for Children, 1999). An adorable rhyming book for all ages.

Down by the Station by Jennifer Riggs Vetter (Tricycle Press, 2009). This play on the old song features sweet illustrations and a plethora of modes of transportation.

Fast Food by Saxton Freymann (Arthur A. Levine Books, 2006). The master of food manipulation provides a clever and hilarious look at transportation. Children will enjoy guessing the different food items.

Freight Train by Donald Crews (Greenwillow, 1978). This simple book combines colors, train cars, and great vocabulary. A must-read for all ages.

Goodnight, Goodnight, Construction Site by Sherri Duskey Rinker and Tom Lichtenheld (Chronicle Books, 2011). A rhyming story about construction vehicles getting ready for "bed."

Honk Honk! Beep Beep! by Daniel Kirk (Disney/Hyperion Books, 2010). A rhyming story with a repeating refrain and large, adorable, Lego-like illustrations.

Hush Little Digger by Ellen Olson-Brown (Tricycle Press, 2006). This funny retake on the mockingbird song features many different working vehicles.

I'm Fast! by Kate McMullen (Balzer and Bray, 2012). Children will thrill at the race between the car and the train. And everyone will love the playful vocabulary.

I've Been Working on the Railroad, edited by Ann Owen (Picture Window Books, 2003). An interesting introduction and the use of just one verse make this a nice addition to storytimes with a wide age range among attendees.

It's Funny Where Ben's Train Takes Him by Robert Burleigh (Orchard Books, 1999). A rhyming story about a young boy and the train adventures that he creates for himself. The repeating line will help involve the children in telling the story.

Machines Go to Work by William Low (Henry Holt, 2009). Every other page poses a question about some form of transportation or another, making this a highly interactive and nicely illustrated storytime book.

Tugga-Tugga Tugboat by Kevin Lewis (Hyperion Books for Children, 2006). Tugboats are almost as interesting as dinosaurs, so this vivid book with its bright illustrations will appeal to children at storytime.

What Do Wheels Do All Day? by April Jones Prince (Houghton Mifflin, 2006). The large format, simple rhyming text, and vivid cut-paper illustrations make this a winner.

Additional Informational Titles

Airport by Byron Barton (Crowell Junior Books, 1982). The spare text and the folksy illustrations make this an excellent choice for storytime.

Big Rigs on the Move by Candice Ransom (Lerner, 2011). Photographs accompany simple text in a book with great appeal for preschoolers.

This Train by Paul Collicutt (Farrar, Straus and Giroux, 2001). Simple text, lots of repetition, and some wonderful math words make this a winner for storytime. Collicutt has many books on different modes of transportation done in this simple style—*This Rocket, This Truck, This Boat, This Plane,* and more.

Additional Poems

"*Rápido* Is Fast" by Jay M. Harris, in *The Moon Is La Luna: Silly Rhymes in English and Spanish* (Houghton Mifflin, 2007), unp.

"Wouldn't You?" by John Ciardi, in *Read-Aloud Rhymes for the Very Young,* edited by Jack Prelutsky (Knopf, 1986), p. 33.

selected references

American Academy of Pediatrics, Council on Communications and Media. 2011. "Policy Statement: Media Use by Children Younger Than 2 Years." *Pediatrics* 128 (5): 1040–45 (e-pub October 17, 2011). doi:10.1542/peds.2011-1753.

Bennett-Armistead, V. Susan. 2005. *Literacy and the Youngest Learner: Best Practices for Educators of Children from Birth to Age 5.* New York: Scholastic.

Center on the Developing Child. 2011. "Building the Brain's 'Air Traffic Control' System: How Early Experiences Shape the Development of Executive Function" (Working Paper No. 11, Harvard University). http://developingchild .harvard.edu.

Copley, Juanita V. 2007. *Mathematics: The Creative Curriculum Approach.* Washington, DC: Teaching Strategies.

Dickinson, D., and M. Smith. 1994. "Long-Term Effects of Preschool Teacher's Book Readings on Low-Income Children's Vocabulary and Story Comprehension." *Reading Research Quarterly* 29:104–22.

Dickinson, David K., ed. 1994. *Bridges to Literacy: Children, Families and Schools.* Cambridge: Blackwell.

Galinsky, Ellen. 2010. *Mind in the Making: The Seven Essential Life Skills Every Child Needs.* New York: HarperStudio.

Hirsch, Elisabeth S., ed. 1984. *The Block Book.* Washington, DC: National Association for the Education of Young Children (NAEYC).

Jacobs, Gera. 2010. *Reaching Standards and Beyond in Kindergarten: Nurturing Children's Sense of Wonder and Joy in Learning.* Thousand Oaks, CA: Corwin and NAEYC.

JAMA and *Archives* Journals. 2007. "Block-Play May Improve Language Development in Toddlers." *ScienceDaily* (October 14; e-pub February 13, 2012).

Neuman, Susan B., et al. 2000. *Learning to Read and Write: Developmentally Appropriate Practices for Young Children.* Washington, DC: NAEYC.

Pratt, Caroline. 1948. *I Learn from Children: An Adventure in Progressive Education.* New York: Simon and Schuster.

Richert, Rebekah A., Michael B. Robb, Jodi G. Fender, and Ellen Wartella. 2010. "Word Learning from Baby Videos." *Archives of Pediatrics and Adolescent Medicine* 164 (5): 432–37 (e-pub March 1, 2010). doi:10.1001/archpediatrics.2010.24.

Schickedanz, Judith A. 1999. *Much More Than ABC's: The Early Stages of Reading and Writing.* Washington, DC: NAEYC.

———. 2008. *Increasing the Power of Instruction: Integration of Language, Literacy, and Math across the Preschool Day.* Washington, DC: NAEYC.

Washington, Valora, ed. 2010. *Children of 2020: Creating a Better Tomorrow.* Washington, DC: Council for Professional Recognition, NAEYC.

Wellhousen, Karyn, and Judith E. Kieff. 2001. *A Constructivist Approach to Block Play in Early Childhood.* Albany, NY: Delmar.

Wilburne, Jane M., et al. 2011. *Cowboys Count, Monkeys Measure, and Princesses Problem Solve: Building Early Math Skills through Storybooks.* Baltimore: Paul H. Brooks.

Williams, Robert A., et al. 2010. *The Preschool Scientist: Using Learning Centers to Discover and Explore Science.* Silver Spring, MD: Gryphon House.

Zimmerman, F. J., D. A. Christakis, and A. N. Meltzoff. 2007. "Associations between Media Viewing and Language Development in Children under Age 2 Years." *Journal of Pediatrics* 151 (4): 364–68 (e-pub August 7, 2007).

index

Titles of books are shown in italic.
Titles of poems are shown in quotes.